PENGUIN BOOKS
THE ESSENTIAL KERALA COOKBOOK

Vijayan Kannampilly is an artist and writer. While he enjoys cooking, he finds the history and culture of the different cuisines, both in India and abroad, equally fascinating.

He lives in Kochi and Delhi.

THE ESSENTIAL KERALA COOKBOOK

Vijayan Kannampilly

PENGUIN BOOKS

PENGUIN BOOKS
Published by the Penguin Group
Penguin Books India Pvt. Ltd, 11 Community Centre, Panchsheel Park,
New Delhi 110 017, India
Penguin Group (USA) Inc., 375 Hudson Street, New York, New York 10014,
USA
Penguin Group (Canada), 90 Eglinton Avenue East, Suite 700, Toronto,
Ontario, M4P 2Y3, Canada (a division of Pearson Penguin Canada Inc.)
Penguin Books Ltd, 80 Strand, London WC2R 0RL, England
Penguin Ireland, 25 St Stephen's Green, Dublin 2, Ireland (a division of Penguin
Books Ltd)
Penguin Group (Australia), 250 Camberwell Road, Camberwell, Victoria
3124, Australia (a division of Pearson Australia Group Pty Ltd)
Penguin Group (NZ), 67 Apollo Drive, Rosedale, Auckland 0632,
New Zealand (a division of Pearson New Zealand Ltd)
Penguin Group (South Africa) (Pty) Ltd, 24 Sturdee Avenue, Rosebank,
Johannesburg 2196, South Africa

Penguin Books Ltd, Registered Offices: 80 Strand, London WC2R 0RL,
England

First published in India by Penguin Books India 2003

Copyright © Vijayan Kannampilly 2003

All rights reserved

22 21 20 19 18 17 16

ISBN 9780143029502

Typeset in Sabon by Mantra Virtual Services, New Delhi
Printed at Akash Press, New Delhi

Contents

Acknowledgements

This book would not have been possible without the advice, assistance and recipes provided so generously by Sara Joseph. I thank her deeply for her kindness of spirit.

Devi Bharathan, Ayisha Mohammed, Lissie George, Chandralekha Shenoy, Shalini Jayaprakash and Resmi Sunil contributed recipes specific to the different communities that make up the mosaic called Kerala; K. Sreedharan and K. Bharathan answered questions and cleared doubts; Aruna Ghose gave books and advice; Ammu Kannampilly and Ravi Ahmad provided research assistance; Ajay Kumar did the initial keying in; Vijander Singh Rawat transformed a muddled up typescript into a readable one; and Sherna Wadia edited it into shape.

I thank all of them.

Introduction

CASTES, CUISINES AND CONFLUENCE
A Brief Note on Malayali Culinary History

What we choose to eat or refuse to eat, and how we eat it defines us as much as our culture and language. If we are what we eat, then the Other is what he is because of what he eats or refuses to eat. Cuisine creates a community; it also keeps communities apart. Food defines, both positively and negatively. Unfortunately, barring a few exceptions and despite the path-breaking work of the late Achaya, the dialectics of food, as culture, as cause and effect of socio-economic changes, as history, has not exercised the minds of most scholars. The indifference is a pan-Indian phenomenon. The history of Malayali food remains unwritten, despite the coming of age of a whole new generation of talented historians. What follows is at best, a sketchy outline, some speculation and one conclusion.

Malayali cuisine as we experience it today is a coming together of three different traditions—Hindu, Christian and Muslim. Though all of them are made up of sub-denominational and regional practices and tastes, the Hindu tradition also has caste differentiations and overtones. Thus while the vegetarian cuisine of the Namputhiris and Nairs do not differ on the whole, the Namputhiris and the Ambalavasis (those who perform ritualistic roles in temples) also abjure garlic, onion and shallot. Within the Hindu culinary tradition there also exist the cuisines of two other vegetarian communities of emigrants—the Tamil Brahmins and the Konkani Gauda Saraswats. While the former group has more or less adopted the Namputhiri-Nair cuisine, the latter has retained its cuisine with subtle incorporations of local produces and some stylistic variations.

Despite the vegetarianism of the Namputhiri-Nair cuisine and the caste hegemony exercised by them, the majority of Malayalis, at present and in the past, are non-vegetarians with a catholicity of taste that now includes beef. At this point it is important to stress that non-vegetarianism in Kerala does not imply (as in the West) that the main course or the heart of the meal is a meat or fish preparation. The typical middle-class Malayali meal today consists of parboiled rice eaten with a gravy of vegetables and pulses, with a complement of dry vegetable preparations, pappadum, pickles *and* a fish or meat dish. This is true for all non-vegetarians. In fact, a meal at any roadside restaurant or teashop would be just this.

The word 'kari' in Malayalam though written as 'curry' in English does not always mean a dish with gravy. It means a pungent, spicy meat or vegetable preparation. (One exception to the general rule is madhura kari, a Muslim sweet dish.) In Malayalam it also means a pickle. The other meaning is anger. Kari also has a literary side. When the Namputhiris used to perform the dance Sangha Kali at a feast, a set of verses called the kari slokam extolling the specialties served at the feast was a part of the performance! The word kari in fact comes from the Tamil word for black pepper, the favoured flavouring while preparing meat and fish dishes. The English transformed the word to mean a spicy dish with gravy.

In Malayali cuisine the kari has two forms—ozhichhukootan kari and thottukootan kari. The first means curries like, pulinkari, pulisseri and sambar that have gravies and the second are dry. As a rule the meat or fish dish with daily meals is a thottukootan kari. In a specific cultural sense this means that most Malayalis do not have any inhibitions about eating fish or meat.

It is in the cooking of meat, poultry and fish that the Malayali makes full use of the produce of the Spice Coast. For this they have to thank the culinary genius of the Christian and Muslim communities of the state. Unlike the rest of India, Kerala's caste system was notable for the absence of an identifiable Vaishya or trading caste. This, plus the mercantile skills and entrepreneurial talents of the Christians and Muslims, made them natural entrants into the spice and other trades and the forerunners of an indigenous mercantile community. In fact, at least two spices which are now associated with Malayali cuisine—clove and nutmeg—came through trade originally from the Spice Islands, Malacca, now called Maluku, and later more extensively through the Dutch.

Unlike North Indian vegetarian cuisine, in the preparation of vegetables the Malayali's reach, as a rule, does not extend beyond pepper, cumin and chillies. Traditionally, the use of spices, barring pepper and some of the green spices, were confined mostly to the preparation of Ayurvedic medicines.

The humble chilli too, has a foreign connection. Achaya points out the word for chilli in most Indian languages is an extension of the word for pepper. The Malayalam mulaku for chilli is derived from the Tamil word milagu for pepper, while pepper itself in the land of pepper becomes kuru-mulaku, meaning seed chilli! Before the introduction

3

of chillies, pepper was extensively used to flavour dishes and it was the key commodity of the spice trade.

External influences are also evident in the biryani, cereal preparations and breads of Malayali Muslim cuisine. All these came through trade contacts with West Asia, and became what it is today by absorbing native culinary techniques.

According to Thangam Philip, Dutch influence is evident in Christian cooking. She says that appam is a variation of the Dutch pancake with coconut milk, the achappam a derivation from Dutch cookies, while puttu is a native dish. Though foreign influences could have contributed to the evolution of appam and achappam, according to Achaya there are descriptions of these dishes (and also of idiappam) in Sangam literature.

Other notable dishes that have entered the Malayali menu from across the seas is the stew made with seafood or vegetables, and the moily that occupies pride of place in most restaurants serving Kerala cuisine. Many Malayalis may find this difficult to digest, but the fact remains that no major Malayalam dictionary has an entry under the word 'moily' or any of its plausible variations. However, in Portuguese 'molho' means dressing or sauce. Another view is that 'moily' is a corruption of Malaya from where the practise of cooking seafood in coconut milk is believed to have come to India.

Every Malayali associates the coconut palm and tapioca with the land and its cuisine. The first came to Kerala over the ocean from the Polynesian Islands. The entry of tapioca into Kerala was the result of a royal decree. Maharaja Visakham Thirunal (1880-1885) of Travancore ordered the cultivation of tapioca from cuttings brought in from Latin America through Africa to ward off a famine.

While Malayali cuisine has over centuries assimilated foreign produces and culinary practices, there are also rather strange exceptions. For instance, despite the West Asian influence, it does not have any meat preparation that has the robustness or the delicacy of the kabab, though there are quite a few references to spit-roasting in Sangam literature. One reason could be that the majority living within the rigid framework of a highly caste-conscious society shunned this method of cooking because it was favoured by the aborigines.

Caste and cuisine have had (and still has) a strong relationship in India. However, in Kerala the structure of the varna system and the rules regarding the inter-relationships within it have been different. In some senses radically so.

Since trade was critical to the revenue of the different kingdoms the entry of Christians and Muslims into the world of commerce was more than welcome. Perhaps this is one factor that has contributed to the higher level of communal tolerance in Hindu majority-Kerala as compared to the rest of India. It also had a great impact on the development of Malayali non-vegetarian cuisine. The essence of this cuisine is its imaginative and delicate use of spices. Or to put it more graphically, even though this cuisine has all the spices it wants growing literally in its backyard, it uses them sparingly as compared to most other non-vegetarian, oriental cuisines.

This act of restraint, this avoidance of exuberance is very much rooted in the Malayali psyche. What is true for most of the Dravida culture—a love for exuberant decoration, for the grand gesture—is avoided, and more often than not, looked down upon by the Malayali aesthete. This approach can be seen in Kerala's traditional architecture and textiles where a minimal use of basic elements, often simple geometry, produces a complex harmony that is deceptively simple, and in the percussion music where a simple base rhythm is literally twisted, stretched and folded over many times to create a perfectly poised equation of delicate balance. The guiding philosophy of Malayali cuisine is not dissimilar. It aspires to produce a harmonious balance through a sparing use of ingredients and by simple methods of preparation. In its essence, it is a minimalist cuisine whether vegetarian or non-vegetarian.

The vast majority in Hindu society living outside the varna system were non-vegetarians, eating mainly fish and game because, as the sixteenth century Portuguese traveller Duarte Barbosa noted, there was 'little breeding of flocks and herds'. Within the varna system itself only the hereditary rulers, the Namputhiris and the Ambalavasis were strict vegetarians. The Nairs were mostly non-vegetarian except in the food that was served at a sadya or feast and at auspicious occasions. The rules of caste not only forbade eating together but had various other restrictions regarding with whom and where one could eat and what each caste could eat. It was because of the severity and inhumanity of rules like these that one of the first social movements led by the progressives in Kerala was to hold what was called communal dining—of people from different castes breaking the caste taboo by eating together in public.

Caste restrictions also extended to what each caste could eat. For instance, though a person outside the varna system could feed a cow, he had no right to milk it, or over its produce, because he would pollute the animal. And to kill a cow was to invite capital punishment in the most gruesome way of being impaled alive. Hence the non-vegetarianism of the Malayali did not extend in those days, at least publicly, to beef. That it does today, is an indication of how much progress has been made in breaking taboos.

Cuisine, in short, had an inclusive and exclusive role. Both the roles had elaborate rules to provide an ideological framework, and one determinant was non-vegetarianism. Given the relationship between caste and cuisine it is not surprising that the challenge to the caste system was also mounted on the same front. This was done by the great social reformer Sree Narayana Guru (1856-1929) who belonged to the Ezhava caste. Existing outside the varna system this caste, numerically the largest in Kerala, was non-vegetarian. Further, non-vegetarianism extended even to feasts held on auspicious occasions. Sree Narayana Guru called for a change in this practice, linking vegetarianism to auspicious occasions. Although it was very much within Hindu tradition and practice it was also a challenge to orthodox Hinduism because it overthrew the taboo on eating the food of the upper castes. It also gave an impetus to the socio-political reformist movement in Kerala mounted by various organizations on different fronts which not only removed the walls of indifference, intolerance and ignorance between castes but also between communities.

At the level of culinary practice it had a major impact. The classical model of Malayali vegetarian cuisine symbolised by the Namputhiri-Nair form of the sadya lost its caste exclusivity. It gained wider acceptance and in the process came to symbolize for the Malayalis the vital expression and essence of their cuisine.

One great symbol of this is the sadya held for the Onam festival. The menu is traditional and vegetarian wherever it is held in the world. In fact the word 'sadya' to most

Malayalis no longer means the form of feast that was once restricted to the Namputhiri and Nair castes; they have made it their very own. This, in my view, has been the greatest revolution in Malayali culinary practice in recent times. It is cuisine at its inclusive best.

A MENU FOR A MONARCH
The Sadya and Other Feasts

Onam (August/September) is the pre-eminent festival in Kerala. The story behind this festival goes like this . . . Once upon a time the asura monarch Mahabali ruled Kerala. His rule was so benign that the devas became jealous and fearful that his subjects would turn away from them. To prevent this Vishnu re-incarnated himself as Vamana, a Brahmin dwarf, tricked Mahabali and banished him to the netherworld.

But before leaving, Mahabali extracted a promise from Vishnu that each year he could return to inquire after the well-being of his subjects. The Onam festival celebrates the annual return of Mahabali.

At the core of the festival is the Onam sadya in which the unseen guest of honour is Mahabali. The primacy of this sadya can be gauged from an old Malayalam saying which advocates even the selling of a mortgaged land in order to eat the Onam sadya! And all other sadya are but variations of this one. There are minor variations in the content and serving of the sadya between regions, and what is given below is specific to central Kerala. Though there are intra-regional variations, the set mode in a region is treated as sacrosanct.

Within the sadya there are two primary classifications—the nalukootan sadya and ettukootan sadya. The first refers to a sadya with four kari and the second to one where eight kari are served. The four kari are, istoo, avial, erisseri and kalan. The remaining four, which make up the eight are olan, pachadi, kichadi and kootukari. Some of these can be paired in terms of taste. Thus istoo and olan have much in common, and so do erisseri and kootukari, and pachadi and kichadi. Avial and kalan are the exceptions. All these are thottukootan kari. The gravy to mix with the rice is provided by an ozhichhukootan kari like sambar or pulisseri.

The sadya is always served on a banana leaf, and the style of serving follows critically important rules. Apart from rice, sambar and pulisseri all the other dishes are placed on the leaf before the guests are seated and they have a fixed place on the leaf, any deviation from which invites rather rude comments. The spine of the banana leaf is taken as the central dividing line. The narrow end of the leaf is on the guest's left.

Pickles and chutneys are placed on the extreme left below the dividing line. Two chutneys and two pickles are served at a full-course sadya. The chutneys are pulinji and injithairu and the pickles comprise chethumanga kari and a lime pickle. These four pickles are rarely ever served except at a sadya. One reason why they are included is that the sweet-sour pulinji, the chilli-ginger-curd flavoured injithairu and the spicy hot-sour lime and mango pickles complement each other and the other dishes rather well. The other is that these easy-to-make pickles and chutneys allow the cooks to spend their time, energy and skills on preparing the more complicated dishes. The third reason, I speculate, could be that the dark brown pulinji, the white injithairu and the red lime and mango pickles present an inviting sight on a green banana leaf!

Above the pickles and chutneys on the other side of the dividing line, pappadum, plantain chips (two savoury and one sweet), savoury elephant foot yam chips and a ripe banana are placed. The banana is generally the short, sweet kadalipazham. If this is not in season then ripe plantains steamed in their skins and cut into five to six centimetre pieces are served. Pappadum are of two types differentiated by their circumference and weight. While the smaller type is always available, shops stock the larger ones only during Onam. During the rest of the year (for instance, for a wedding feast) they have to be specially ordered. The pappadum are always placed over the chips without covering them entirely.

All the kari are served above the dividing line. The first is istoo. This is placed at least seven centimetres to the right of the pappadum, chips and banana. After istoo comes olan, pachadi, kichadi, avial, erisseri, kootukari and kalan. They are placed in a row with a little space between each, except for the kalan, which is placed three centimetres or so below them. This is to prevent the sweet-sour kalan from mixing with the other kari and killing their taste. Below the dividing line and on the extreme right, salt and a pigeon pea dish (cooked with ghee and salt) is placed.

While the order remains the same for a four-kari sadya, some of the kari indicated earlier, plus two chutneys, one pickle, large pappadum, ripe banana and two salty chips are generally dropped.

The rice is served after the guests are seated. The serving utensil for rice is woven out of split bamboo and is cylindrical. The rice is served by jerking the basket in a smooth motion. No ladles or spoons are used.

The first mouthful of rice is generally eaten with the

pigeon peas mainly to clear the palate, and so the portion of the pigeon peas is extremely small. The next dish to be served is sambar. This is poured onto the rice. As the feasting proceeds, the other kari are eaten more or less according to personal preferences. However, a gourmet would proceed from left to right because there is a definite progression in taste from the mild and smooth istoo to the slightly pungent and gritty erisseri. Again kalan is the exception. The second helping of rice is accompanied by rasam—an import from Tamil Nadu—and finally the payasam.

In an eight-kari sadya two payasam are served. The first is sweetened with jaggery and has a coconut milk base and the second is sweetened with sugar and has a milk base. If the sadya is of a lesser order, then the sugar-based payasam is dropped. Often the banana and pappadum are eaten with the jaggery payasam. While the banana can be eaten with the sugar-based payasam, pappadum are never eaten with this. The serving of the payasam is generally viewed as the high point of the culinary journey by most Malayalis. So much so, that even households that do not prepare the whole course for an Onam sadya would still make a payasam.

This fascination with payasam is rather puzzling. Cuisine north of the Vindhyas boasts of many sweet dishes remarkable for their different flavours, textures and shapes. By and large they are culinary manifestations of milk. The South performs a similar miracle by turning rice into a variety of savouries and snacks.

Malayali cuisine is an exception to this. While dosai, idli and vada are borrowings, appam, pathiri and puttu are too heavy to be called savouries or snacks in the true sense of the meaning. On the other hand, Malayali cuisine actually places a lot of emphasis on imparting a very high level of sweetness to the payasam. So much so, that in a sadya it is customary to serve lime or mango pickle on the side after the payasam are served. The pickle is used much like a sorbet to clear the palate. This poses a puzzle. Why did a people who have such a pronounced sweet tooth fail to develop a wider variety of sweet dishes? The answer perhaps lies in milk, the basic ingredient in India for sweet dishes. The 'little breeding of herds' that Barbosa had noted could not have allowed for a milk-surplus economy. The other was the caste restrictions on milk consumption.

After the payasam, a helping of rice with curd is served. This is regarded as a digestive and to clear the palate. With this the sadya ends. Etiquette demands that the guests move all that is left over to the centre of the top half of the leaf and fold the bottom half over it.

Feasts to celebrate other festivals, birthdays, marriages, naming ceremonies of newborn children, and wakes held after the death of family members are similar to the sadya except in the deletions from the menu. Thus in a Hindu wake pappadum are never served. Interestingly, both Hindus and Christians are strict vegetarians for a short period after a death in the family.

Though epitomising the Malayali banquet, the sadya has not erased other forms and types of feasts like those particular to Muslims and Christians.

In a Muslim feast held to celebrate a marriage, the service would start with a welcoming drink of lime juice, followed by alisa, then ghee rice, chicken curry and pigeon pea curry. After this come the sweet dishes—muttamala and pathiri made with Bengal gram. The last course is a dish of banana and pineapple pieces sprinkled with pepper powder and sugar, similar to the fruit chat of North India.

The menu for celebrating festivals like Id would include ghee rice with chicken, mutton or pigeon pea curry, a chutney made with coconut, green chillies, garlic, shallots, vinegar and salt, pappadum and a sweet dish like madhura kari. Muslims break their fast by eating dry fruits and drinking broths flavoured with fenugreek, cumin and red mustard (rai) or a sweet liquid pudding like thari kachiyathu. The two meals between ten at night and four in the morning are puttu or pathiri with curries, and rice with curries.

In a Christian marriage feast the first course is appam with either a fish moily or mapas. After this, duck, chicken or mutton fried with potatoes and beans is served. The main course is rice with fish curry, vegetable thoran, pickles, pappadum and buttermilk seasoned with spices and lemon leaves. The dessert is a thick rice payasam sweetened with jaggery. Coffee and tea are served after the meal.

Most Malayali Christians abstain from meat and fish from the first of December until after the midnight mass on the twenty-fourth. The fast is broken with a heavy breakfast at around six o'clock on Christmas morning. The menu consists of appam, meat mapas, mutton fry, chicken peralen, roast duck, wheat halva and steamed plantain. Latin Christians (those who converted to Christianity after the arrival of the Portuguese) also serve wine and cakes.

For Christmas lunch the starter is appam with beef mapas. This is followed by rice with duck curry, fish fry or curry, chicken varatiathu, vegetable thoran, pappadum, pickles, curd and halva. Buttermilk seasoned with spices is served as a drink. Dinner is traditionally considered unimportant.

On Maundy Thursday it is customary among most Christian communities to make a steamed, unsweetened cake from rice which is not parboiled, black beans, cumin, shallots, garlic, coconut and salt. The cake is decorated with a piece of fresh turmeric and a small cross made out of a piece of palm leaf sanctified in the church. The cake, called inri appam (as in I.N.R.I., the abbreviated inscription on the Cross) in Malayalam, is eaten with a dip made of jaggery syrup and coconut milk. The symbolic connection to the Last Supper is evident.

EARTH, STONE AND METAL
The Cooking Utensils of Kerala

The best known Malayali cooking utensil is the uruli made of bell metal. It is circular, squat and wide-mouthed and comes in many sizes. The other metallic utensils are the charakku, a large round cauldron with handles on either side of the rim, and the vaarpu, a large pan made of bronze. All these utensils are used to make payasam, sambar and kari, except kalan, pachadi and kichadi, and chutneys and pickles as they are sour. These dishes are made in a kalchatti, carved out of soft stone, with a mouth wider than its base. Generally, a kalchatti is a tall utensil with the height being more than the circumference.

The uruli, charakku and kalchatti get hot gradually and retain heat for some time, hence they are used for cooking everything except rice.

Charakku

In a sadya the volume of work demands that all the dishes are cooked more than an hour or so before the guests are seated, while kalan is generally cooked the previous night so that it matures well. Rice

Vaarpu

however is cooked last. It is timed in such a manner that it can be served literally straight off the fire! The other reason is that the requirement of rice in sheer quantity, is much more than all the other dishes put together! Hence, in a large sadya rice is cooked many times. The cooking of rice is done in a chembu, a low, wide-mouthed utensil made of copper—a metal that heats quickly. Incidentally, the quantities of all ingredients required for a sadya are measured in relationship to the quantity of rice that has to be cooked.

Various long-handled metal spatulas of different types are used for stirring payasam and sambar. Generally wooden ladles are used for the vegetables so as not to bruise them and to transfer rice from the chembu into the serving baskets.

Fish is cooked in a terracotta, flat-bottomed, open-mouthed vessel called the meenchatti (meaning, cooking utensil for fish). Before putting a meenchatti to use it is necessary to boil water in it and drain it out at least thrice. At the third time, a tablespoon of refined oil can be added to the water. This helps to remove all traces of clay and seals the pores of the chatti.

The Malayali style of preparing fish generally calls for slow cooking. This leads to two problems. The curry could easily brown and stick to the base of the chatti and stirring it could lead to the disintegration of the fish. Holding the rim of the chatti with both hands and swirling the curry around prevents these dreadful mishaps. The structure and design of the chatti allows for all these. It retains heat inside for a long time (thus allowing for slow cooking) and remains just warm enough on the outside, to permit the gentle swirling. If stirring is unavoidable then what the Malayali uses is the handle of a wooden ladle.

The kadhai is used for all stir-fried dishes and for deep frying. In Malayalam the kadhai is called cheenachatti. The word 'cheena' means China and Chinese in Malayalam. The fact that the kadhai known as the wok is essential to Chinese culinary practice indicates that the cheenachatti came to Kerala from across the sea through the Chinese trade.

Appachatti

Malayali cuisine also uses the appachatti for making appam, the sevanazhi or idiappam press for idiappam, and the puttukutti for puttu.

The appachatti is shaped like a kadhai or wok except that it comes with a lid, is much smaller, the sides are less steep and it always has a curved base. Traditionally, they were made of terracotta or cast iron. Today, non-stick appachatti are available.

The sevanazhi for making idiappam is a metal tube with a diameter of six to seven centimetres. The base has a circular ridge to hold a disc. There are several of these discs, each with different sized holes in them. The top has a lid with a hole in the centre to hold a piston in place. While the base of the piston is within the tube its rod protrudes out through the hole. A crank attached to the rod enables the user to turn the piston clockwise and push the dough out in strands through the disc. Before making idiappam the appropriate disc is chosen, dough filled into the tube and then the lid with the piston is put in place. The sevanazhi is made in brass or stainless steel.

Puttukutti

The puttukutti is a tubular utensil approximately eighteen to twenty-six centimetres in height with a diameter of six to seven centimetres. A circular ridge at the base holds a disc with holes in it. Rice flour and grated coconut are filled into the tube and a close-fitting cap, with two to three holes in it, is put on the top. The puttukutti is then inserted into a long-necked utensil containing water. The steam from the heated water escapes through the tube and cooks the puttu. Earlier, the puttukutti was made by using a piece of bamboo (a natural tube) of the appropriate size, or bell metal. If bamboo was used a piece of coir rope was wound around it for most of its length. This prevented the bamboo from expanding and cracking in the heat and enabled users to handle it without scorching their hands. Today, the puttukutti is made of stainless steel or aluminium.

PREPARING FOR THE POT
Coconuts and Other Ingredients

There is a widespread belief that the word keralam means the land of coconuts palms or keram. Whether this word origin is accepted or not, the coconut does play an all-pervasive role in Malayali cuisine. Besides enhancing the flavour of the cooked dish it also helps to blend and tone down the potency of the spices.

Sometimes copra (dry coconut) is used, but by and large it is the fresh, mature one that is used. The husk of freshly plucked coconuts have a greeny brown or golden yellow colour. The meat is juicy and yields milk easily. The longer the plucked coconut remains unused, the browner the husk gets and it develops a shrivelled look. The meat of a coconut in this condition yields very little milk, nor is it good for cooking.

Before the coconut matures, the flesh is very tender and creamy and the water content is higher. The flesh is eaten as a snack and the water is taken as a beverage. Tender coconuts are not generally used for cooking.

TO GRATE COCONUT

The manual grater used in Kerala is a metal blade with sawed edges mounted on a low stool. If you do not have a manual grater, you can always use a hand-held grater or cut the coconut meat into small pieces and use the grating blade of a food processor.

To prise coconut meat from the shell use the tip of a sharp knife to score through the inside of the coconut in concentric circles, about a centimetre apart. Then score the meat from the bottom to the top, keeping at least five centimetres between the knife markings. Finally, insert the tip of the knife between the shell and the meat to prise the two apart.

TO GRIND COCONUT

Controlling the consistency of the coconut while it is being ground is of supreme importance in Malayali cuisine. Different dishes require different consistencies. A lavish sadya calls for a large number of coconuts to be ground. Hence, the first major culinary activity for a sadya is to grind the coconuts according to the requirements of the master chef. Very often grinding coconuts is a female activity. In fact, to ease the tedium of grinding and probably to impart a rhythm to their action, women (especially in North Kerala) sing special songs on the occasion.

To grind coconut follow these basic rules:

- When the recipe calls for coarse or rough grinding do not use water.
- To get a fine paste add 1½ cups water for one coconut.
- Extra fine paste does not require more water. Just grind for a longer time until you get a creamy consistency.

It is presumed that you will be using an electric grinder or food processor. If you are using a grinding stone then the amount of water required should be reduced considerably.

COCONUT MILK

Makes: ½ cup 1st extract; 1 cup 2nd extract; and 2 cups 3rd extract

To make coconut milk the Malayali way:

1 medium-sized, fresh coconut, grated

1st extract:
- Sprinkle ½ cup cold water over coconut gratings.
- Squeeze out milk to get the first milk or extract (thalapal).

2nd extract:
- Add 1 cup cold water to the squeezed coconut gratings and squeeze out milk to get the second extract (randampal).

3rd extract:
- Repeat with 2 cups cold water to get the third extract (moonnampal).

To use canned coconut milk:
- The undiluted milk serves as the 1st extract.
- Dilute 1 cup milk with 1 cup water and use as the 2nd extract.
- Dilute 1 cup milk with 2 cups water and use as the 3rd extract.

Note: While using 3 extracts of coconut milk in cooking, the 3rd extract is added first, then the 2nd and finally the 1st. This is necessary for slow cooking, especially for a payasam.

Hot or warm water is never sprinkled on fresh coconut gratings to get the first extract. Anything hot or warm (including an oven) will increase the oil flavour in the coconut meat and kill the delicacy of the coconut milk.

While using canned coconut milk, make sure to shake the tin before opening it, or whisk the milk well before using.

COOKING MEDIUM

The cooking medium of Malayali cuisine is coconut oil. Whether this was always the case, or whether coconut oil supplanted sesame oil is a moot point. In Malayalam, coconut oil is called velichenna, a compound of two words, 'velicham' meaning light, and 'enna' meaning oil. Sesame oil is called nallenna, a compound of 'nallathu' meaning good, and 'enna' meaning oil. This may indicate that coconut oil was originally used for lighting purposes and sesame oil for cooking because it was a 'good' oil, i.e. it does not turn rancid (a reason why it is used in all pickles by Malayalis) unlike coconut oil. Finally, while coconut and sesame seeds are used as temple offerings only the latter is used in the rites and rituals of the Namputhiris and Nairs. This religious and ritualistic sanctity attached to sesame seeds, I surmise, indicates its culinary acceptance as an oilseed prior to the currently ubiquitous coconut.

Malayali cuisine does not suffer for the worse if one substitutes refined vegetable oil for coconut oil. In this book coconut oil is by and large given a miss, unless the recipe demands it.

RICE

The staple food of the Malayali is parboiled rice. The rice commonly sold in the markets around the country does not undergo any processing before it is husked from fresh paddy. When the paddy is boiled, dried and then husked, you get parboiled rice. If the husking is done in such a manner that the bran is not completely lost, the cooked rice will have a reddish tone.

To cook this rice you will need five times the quantity of water compared to the quantity of rice. Bring water to boil, add rice, lower heat and cook till rice is soft. Drain rice in a colander.

The water is never thrown away. With a little cooked rice added to it, it becomes congee, a staple breakfast and supper for many Malayalis. Congee is also used as cattle feed.

In a major sadya the congee is drained into a large wooden rectangular tub resembling a small boat buried in the ground because it is easier to lower the heavy chembu than to lift it up. A wooden paddle holds the chembu in place and allows the water to drain out.

Parched rice:
Often used in Kerala, it is an ancient method of eating rice, evidenced by references in Sangam literature. It is prepared by soaking rice grains in water, then roasting them over hot sand till they are ready to puff up. Finally, they are beaten flat in a large mortar and pestle.

CARDAMOM

The cardamoms used in Kerala are white cardamoms. These are actually the small green cardamoms which are bleached in the sun till white or pale yellow.

SOURING AGENTS

There are many souring agents used in Malayali cuisine.

Cambodge:
Cambodge is specific to Malayali fish cuisine. Most writers refer to this as kokum which is used in Goa, the Konkan Coast and by the Kodavas. Kokum (punampuli in Malayalam) is *Garcinia indica*; cambodge (kudampuli in Malayalam) is *Garcinia gummigutta*. Despite the subtle difference in taste kokum can be substituted for cambodge if the latter is unavailable. If kokum too is unavailable use tamarind. You can't go very wrong.

Before reaching the market, the fruit is cut open, its pulpy contents removed and discarded and the outer skin or petals are sun-dried to an even black colour.

Cambodge is stored in air-tight earthenware or porcelain jars or bottles away from sunlight with a handful of salt spread over it to act as a preservative.

To use, tear the petals into 2-3 pieces and soak in water for at least 10-20 minutes. Do not squeeze. Depending on the recipe one can use the pieces with or without the water.

Tamarind:
The word tamarind is an English corruption of the Arabic thamur-ul-Hind, meaning 'dates of India'.

Sometimes seedless tamarind is added directly to the dish. Usually a pulp is made with tamarind.

Soak tamarind in water (the quantities depends on the recipe) and squeeze till it dissolves. Strain and use the dark brown coloured tamarind pulp.

Unripe mango:
Unripe mango is used in some fish and vegetable preparations.

Lime juice and vinegar:
Lime juice is not an important souring agent, but vinegar is used particularly as a souring agent for meat preparations.

Bilimbi:
The fruit of the *Averrhoa bilimbi*, also known as the cucumber tree is used in fish and vegetable preparations. It is also pickled. In Malayalam it is called irumpanpuli.

Curd:
When curd is used in cooking, its main purpose is to provide body to the dish. However it also acts as a mild souring agent.

TEMPERING

Tempering is the last stage in Malayali cooking. There are two reasons for tempering a dish. First, as the name suggests it imparts a certain flavour and piquancy to the dish. Secondly, dishes that contain no oil get a touch of it.

The basic ingredients used in tempering are oil, mustard seeds, dry red chillies and curry leaves.

Heat oil to smoking point and add mustard seeds. When they start sputtering, add red chillies torn into pieces. Lower heat, as you get the aroma of chillies and add curry leaves. Remove from heat within a minute or so, pour contents of pan into the prepared dish and mix well. If shallots are used in the tempering then chop and add to oil before chillies. Allow to brown and add chillies.

Special small tempering pans are available in the market for this purpose. They have a heavy base and a handle for ease of use. Often the entire pan is plunged into the dish as its contents are poured out. It is then stirred into the dish.

STEAMING

Traditionally a steamer was made of copper since it is a good conductor of heat. It is a deep vessel with a tight-fitting lid. It contains a series of perforated trays, that rest on each other to hold the food. Water is boiled in the steamer and the steam rises through the perforations to cook the food.

Steamer

If you don't have a steamer you can make one by placing a small pan containing the food to be steamed on an inverted metal bowl or katori in a larger pan.

Pour water into the large pan to come halfway up the smaller pan. Cover the large pan with a tight fitting lid. Bring water to boil and keep it boiling for the required time, replenishing it with more boiling water as needed.

THE BANANA LEAF

The banana leaf is used by the Malayali not only to serve food. It is often used as a lid while cooking. Gourmets believe that it enhances the flavour of a dish, especially when preparing a vegetarian dish like avial. It is also used to wrap food before steaming or grilling.

To prepare a banana leaf wrapper clean both sides of the leaf (the reverse side first) using a damp cloth taking care to use a movement perpendicular to the spine. Otherwise the leaf will tear. Pass the leaf over a live flame without allowing it to get scorched. This wilts and softens the leaf.

Use a knife or kitchen scissors to cut away the main vein. The leaf will now be pliable enough to be used as a wrapper. In this book the assumption is that the banana leaf is approximately 30 cm long and 25 cm wide.

MEAT POULTRY AND FISH

Traditionally, meat, poultry and fish were cut rather small as compared to the practice in western cuisine.

There are three obvious reasons behind this method. First, none of these is eaten as a main dish. Secondly, the small size of the pieces allows for better marinating and faster cooking. Finally, the economy imposed by the size permitted a larger number of people to partake of the dish.

Though the recipes adhere to the traditional method of cutting, nothing much will be lost if one were to cut the meat, poultry or fish according to one's preference.

Barring a few exceptions, all vegetable dishes are served with rice. The exceptions are indicated in the relevant recipes. Since these dishes can be either with or without gravy, it is usual to serve a combination of different dishes with a meal. There is no hard and fast rule for determining the combinations, except when it comes to a sadya. Because there is always more than one dish on the table the serving portions, as a rule, are small.

Malayali cuisine uses a variety of vegetables that are either common only to tropical regions or if grown elsewhere are not used so extensively in other cuisines. Given below are the methods used to clean them before cooking.

Tapioca:
This has a thin brown outer skin and a thicker inner white or pink skin. Wash the tapioca, dry and cut to the desired length. Use a sharp knife to peel away both the skins. Split down the middle and use the knife to remove the inner fibre. Soak in water and wash well before using.

Elephant foot yam/Yam:
Cut into convenient-sized pieces. Use a sharp knife and peel the skin at least 3-5 mm deep. Soak in water and wash well before using.

Colocasia/Cherukizhangu:
Use a sharp knife to scrape off or peel skin. Soak in water and wash well before using.

Note: Unless elephant foot yam and colocasia are washed

properly before they are cooked they could give you an itching sensation in the throat.

Pumpkin/Snakegourd/Ashgourd:
Cut into convenient-sized pieces. Peel skin with a sharp knife. Remove and discard the inner soft portion with seeds. Wash and cut.

Drumsticks:
Wash and scrape off green skin with a sharp knife (as you would celery) and cut.

Drumstick leaves:
Before the drumstick leaves can be used their stalks have to be removed. An easy, modern method is to pull the leaves off the branch and put them, stalks and all, into a polythene bag. Place the bag overnight in a refrigerator. The next day the stalks will come off easily from the leaves.

Banana Flower:
Remove and discard outer cover and petals till you reach the white inner part. It is this that is cooked.

Malabar Catmint or Coleus Tuber:
Known as koorka in Malayalam, this tuber is approximately 3 cm long with a girth of about 2 cm. The leaves of the plant look similar to mint leaves and have an aroma that cats like! The tuber has a dark brown thin outer skin. This has to be removed before cooking. Given the small size, scraping off the skin is not an easy task. Hence, the preferred method is to soak it in water for an hour and then wrap it in a piece of coarse jute cloth. Use an abrasive rolling motion or beat it against the floor to

loosen the skin. Scrape it off with a knife. Wash before using.

Jackfruit/Breadfruit:
There are two varieties of jackfruit. In one the flesh of the fruit is firm and sweet. Known as varikkachakka this is preferred for cooking. The other variety is pulpy when mature and is mainly eaten as a fruit.

Before cooking cut the jackfruit into convenient sized pieces. Use a very sharp knife to cut away the outer, spiky skin and then the inner skin. Rub oil onto to your palms to insulate them from the gummy extrusion from the jackfruit. Pluck out the golden yellow fruit. Take care to remove the fibres that secure the fruit to the skin. Rub a little oil on the extracted fruit to remove the gummy extrusion.

Remove seeds. They can be stored and used later. Before using scrape off the outer skin with a knife.

Unlike the jackfruit, breadfruit is smaller and does not have a spiky skin.

Plantain:
Plantains are part of the banana family with a subtle difference. Unripe plantains can be cooked as a vegetable while the ripe ones can be eaten like a fruit. As a rule the nenthrakkaya or plantain is 3 cm in girth and 15 cm in length. They have to be peeled before they are used except when they are steamed.

Onions and Shallots:
Two types of onions are used in Malayali cooking. One is the large-sized one known as pyaz (*Allium cepa*) in Hindi. The other is the shallot (*Allium ascalonicum*), commonly called sambar onion or Madras onion.

Shallots are generally available in South Indian shops. They have a flavour that is subtler than onions.

Though onions can be substituted for shallots one should also be prepared for a loss in flavour.

One onion is equivalent to about eight shallots.

Chillies:
Though Malayalis in general prefer pungent dishes, there is no hard and fast rule about the level of pungency that a dish should have. In practise, it is a matter of individual preference and the quantity of chillies mentioned in the recipes can be adjusted to taste. They may also be seeded, to get the flavour of the chillies without their pungency.

In a broad sense, the use of chillies (green and dry) is much higher in non-vegetarian dishes because they are believed to have medicinal values and act as a preservative. By slitting, chopping or tearing chillies before adding them to the dish their capsaicin value is reduced.

A variety of chilli that is grown extensively in Kerala and some parts of Tamil Nadu is the kanthari. It is short, white and has a capsaicin value as high as 0.504%. It is generally used in chutneys, and a liberal dose of oil is added to reduce the pungency.

TABLE OF MEASURES

The cup measure used in this book is a 200 ml cup

1 tsp = 5 ml
1 tbsp = 3 tsp
A pinch = 1/8 tsp (literally a pinch)
A dash = 1-2 drops

All spoon measures are level

Note: Scant cup/tbsp/tsp used in the recipes means just a little less than the level measure.

Basic Recipes

MALAYALI FIVE-SPICE POWDER

Makes: 100 gms

This is a name I have coined to make the recipes easy to follow. It is often mistakenly referred to as garam masala in Malayalam, but this spice mix is different. Unlike garam masala, it does not contain pepper. It is extensively used in Malayali Muslim cuisine.

The use of five-spice powder certainly gives a lift to a dish. In some parts of Kerala, cumin, caraway seeds (shah jeera) and cardamoms are also added to the five spices.

The powder has some similarity to the Arab mix, baharat, though this too uses pepper. Chinese cuisine has a five-spice powder which bears no similarity to the one used in Malayali cuisine. Fennel is common to the panch phoron used in Bengali cuisine. Other than that, there is no resemblance.

1 nutmeg, grated or broken into small pieces
100 gms fennel seeds (badi saunf)
10 x 5-cm sticks cinnamon, broken into pieces
10 cloves
2 large flakes mace

- Mix all ingredients together and dry roast lightly for 5 minutes over low heat.
- Cool, grind to a fine powder and store in an airtight bottle.

SAMBAR POWDER

Makes: 200 gms

1 tsp coconut oil
50 gms asafoetida (hing) pieces
50 gms dry red chillies, torn into pieces
1 tsp husked Bengal gram (chana dal)
100 gms coriander seeds
1 tsp fenugreek seeds (methi)

- Heat oil in a frying pan over moderate heat. Add asafoetida, lower heat and add red chillies. Fry for 2 minutes, stirring constantly.
- Sprinkle in remaining ingredients and continue frying, stirring constantly till gram turns golden brown.
- Cool, grind to a fine powder and store in an airtight bottle.

JAGGERY SYRUP

Though jaggery can be added directly to a dish, it is advisable to make it into a syrup to reduce cooking time and for easy removal of impurities.

1 kg jaggery, broken into small pieces

- Place jaggery in a pan with 1 cup water and bring to boil. Stir well and cook till jaggery melts and starts to thicken.
- Remove from heat, cool and strain.

ADA
Rice Flakes

Makes: 1 kg

1 kg sifted rice flour (sift through a fine-meshed sieve and use only the
finest flour)
100 gms unsalted butter
½ tsp salt
25 large banana leaves

- Mix rice flour and butter. Add salt and 2 cups water
  to make a smooth, thick paste. Add a little more water
  if the mixture is too thick.
- Clean banana leaves with a damp cloth on both sides,
  dry and pass over a live flame to make them pliable.
  Cut into suitable sized pieces.
- Spread paste evenly and thinly on banana leaves.
- Roll leaves (like a Swiss roll), fold them in at both ends
  and tie with cotton string to secure.
- Bring plenty of water to boil in a wide pan, immerse
  rolls in water and boil for 10 minutes.
- Remove rolls from pan and drain.
- Open leaves and prise away the semi-cooked rice paste
  (ada), with a knife. Cut into very small flakes, about
  ½-cm in size.
- Rinse ada in cold water, spread on a tray and keep in
  the sun, covered with a thin muslin cloth, till crisp.
- Store in airtight containers and use as required.

Vegetables

The essential characteristic of Malayali vegetarian cuisine is to cook vegetables lightly. Each vegetable, it is believed must be allowed to proclaim its distinct taste and flavour in a dish. Another important quality that a gourmet looks for is the aesthetic presentation of each vegetable. So the rules governing the cutting of vegetables have to be strictly observed.

In addition to the methods used to prepare the eight dishes that comprise the ettukoottam kari served at feasts, the Malayali also uses three other methods. First, the thoran in which the vegetable is stirred and fried or cooked with ground or grated coconut; second, the mezhukkupuratti, that is stir-frying with oil but without coconut; and finally, the puzhukku meaning a thick potage of a starchy tuber or variety of tubers, with peas and pulses.

Two other styles of cooking, theeyal and mapas, are similar to meat and poultry preparations. In the former, spices and coconut are fried and ground (the varatharachakari) before being used, while in the latter ground or whole spices are used with coconut milk.

Most of the principal vegetarian dishes are intrinsic to the Namputhiri-Nair culinary tradition, marked by the absence of fine spices (cloves, cinnamon, etc.) and garlic in the dishes, while in orthodox households even shallots and onions are not used. But, as said earlier, this culinary tradition has become very much a part of the Malayali way of life today with interesting additions and changes brought in by other communities.

NENTHRAKKAYA KALAN
Unripe Plantain Curry with Curd and Coconut

Serves: 8

This preparation is one of the eight dishes served at feasts. It is a delicate and difficult dish to make because the coconut has to be ground to an extra fine paste. The traditional test was to throw a spoonful of the coconut paste at a smooth wall—it should not slide off but stick to the wall. A well-made kalan can keep for a week or so without refrigeration.

2 unripe plantains
4 shallots, chopped
2 green chillies, chopped
½ tsp black pepper powder
1 tsp red chilli powder
½ tsp turmeric powder
1½ tsp salt
2 cups thick curd (not very sour), whisked

Ground to an extra fine paste:
1 medium-sized, fresh coconut, grated
2 shallots, chopped
A pinch of cumin powder
1½ cups water

Tempering:
1½ tbsp coconut oil
1 tsp mustard seeds
1 tsp fenugreek seeds (methi)
2 shallots, chopped
2 stalks curry leaves

- Peel plantains, slit lengthwise and cut into 1-cm cubes.
- Place plantains in a pan with shallots, green chillies, spice powders, salt and ¾ cup water, and cook over low heat for about 10 minutes.
- Stir in curd and simmer for 5 minutes.
- Mix in coconut paste and simmer over low heat till gravy thickens.
- Heat oil for tempering in a small pan and sprinkle in mustard seeds. When they start sputtering, add remaining ingredients and fry till shallots turn brown.
- Pour contents of pan into curry, mix well and serve.

Variation: Kalan can also be made with elephant foot yam (zimikand).

MAMPAZHA KALAN
Sweet Mango Curry with Curd and Coconut

Serves: 8

In Kerala, a mango called chandrakaran is used to prepare this dish. It is small, pulpy and sweet. A north Indian substitute would be the chausa.

500 gms table mangoes
10 green chillies, slit
2 tsp black pepper powder
1 tsp turmeric powder
2 tsp salt
1½ tbsp grated or powdered jaggery
1 litre thick curd (not very sour), whisked
½ tsp fenugreek seeds (methi), lightly fried and powdered

Ground to an extra fine paste:

1 medium-sized, fresh coconut, grated
¼ tsp cumin seeds
1½ cups water

Tempering:

4 tbsp coconut oil
1 tsp mustard seeds
3 dry red chillies, torn into pieces
1 tsp fenugreek seeds (methi)
2 stalks curry leaves

- Wash mangoes, drain well and peel. Keep whole, with seeds intact and reserve skin.
- Soak mango skin in 2½ cups warm water for 30 minutes. Squeeze out water from skin into a pan and discard skin.
- Add mangoes, green chillies, pepper, turmeric, salt, and jaggery to pan and cook over high heat for about 10 minutes, stirring occasionally.
- Stir in curd and continue to cook over high heat for 10 minutes more.
- Lower heat, mix in fenugreek and coconut paste, and simmer over low heat till gravy thickens.
- Heat oil for tempering in a small pan and sprinkle in mustard seeds. When they start sputtering, toss in red chillies and fry for a few moments till fragrant, shaking the pan occasionally. Add remaining ingredients and fry for a few moments longer.
- Pour contents of pan into curry, mix well and serve.

ERISSERI
Yam and Unripe Plantain Curry with Fried Coconut

Serves: 8

This is one of the eight dishes served at all feasts. It is also called elisseri in some parts of Kerala.

500 gms elephant foot yam (zimikand)
250 gms unripe plantains
1 tsp red chilli powder
¼ tsp turmeric powder
1 tsp salt

Ground to a paste:
½ medium-sized, fresh coconut, grated
½ tsp cumin seeds
½ cup water

Tempering:
2 tbsp coconut oil
2 tsp mustard seeds
3 dry red chillies, torn into pieces
½ medium-sized, fresh coconut, grated
3 stalks curry leaves

- Peel yam, wash and cut into 3-cm cubes. Peel and slit plantains lengthwise into half, and cut into 1-cm cubes.
- Place yam, plantains, spice powders and salt in a pan with 1½ cups water, and cook over high heat for 20 minutes.
- Mix in coconut paste and bring to boil. Lower heat and cook till gravy thickens.
- Heat oil for tempering in a small pan and sprinkle in mustard seeds. When they start sputtering, toss in red

41

chillies and fry for a few moments till fragrant, shaking the pan occasionally. Add remaining ingredients and fry, stirring constantly, till coconut turns brown.
• Pour contents of pan into curry, mix well and serve.

Variations: Erisseri can also be made with the following combinations:

• Mature jackfruit, pumpkin and pigeon peas (arhar/ toover dal)
• Pumpkin and green beans (moong) or pigeon peas
• Drumstick leaves and pigeon peas
• Pigeon peas.

KOOTUKARI
Yam, Unripe Plantain and Bengal Gram Curry

Serves: 8

In north Kerala, it is mandatory to serve this dish at feasts. To my knowledge, in south and central Kerala kootukari is served only when the feast is of a high order, calling for ettukoottam kari or eight dishes. The cutting of vegetables is governed by strict rules. For this dish, the yam and plantain should be cut into 1-cm cubes.

1½ cups whole Bengal gram (kala chana)
4 unripe plantains
250 gms elephant foot yam (zimikand)
10 black peppercorns, powdered
¼ tsp turmeric powder
2 dry red chillies, torn into pieces
1 tsp salt

Ground to a paste:

> 1 medium-sized, fresh coconut, grated
> ¼ tsp cumin seeds
> ½ cup water

Tempering:

> 2 tbsp oil
> 1 tsp mustard seeds
> 2 tbsp husked black beans (urad dal)
> 6 dry red chillies, torn into pieces
> ½ medium-sized, fresh coconut, grated

- Wash gram and soak overnight in water.
- Peel and cut plantains and yam into 1-cm cubes.
- Drain gram and rinse. Place in a pan with 1½ cups fresh water and cook over high heat for about 30 minutes.
- Add plantains, yam, spice powders and red chillies, and cook over moderate heat for about 15 minutes till yam is tender.
- Stir in salt and continue to cook till nearly dry.
- Remove from heat, mix in coconut paste, and set aside.
- Heat oil for tempering in a small pan and sprinkle in mustard seeds. When they start sputtering, add dal and fry till red. Toss in red chillies and fry for a few moments till fragrant, shaking the pan occasionally. Mix in coconut and fry, stirring constantly, till coconut turns brown.
- Pour contents of pan into curry, mix well and serve.

ISTOO
Potato Stew

Serves: 6

Istoo is the Malayalam corruption of 'stew'. It is a part of the menu for feasts but can also served with appam and idiappam. The stew can be made with various combinations of ingredients which are usually indicated in the name of the dish, except when it is made only with potatoes, when it is called just istoo.

2 medium-sized potatoes, peeled and cut into 5-cm cubes
1 medium-sized onion, chopped
10 green chillies, slit
3-cm piece ginger, chopped
1 tsp black pepper powder
1 tsp salt
1 cup coconut milk (1st extract; see p. 20)
1 stalk curry leaves
2 tbsp oil

- Place potatoes, onion, green chillies, ginger, pepper, salt and ¾ cup water in a pan over moderate heat and cook till potatoes are tender enough to break lightly into smaller pieces with a ladle.
- Stir in coconut milk and curry leaves and heat through for a minute.
- Heat oil and pour it in. Mix well and serve.

Variations:
Pachakari Istoo (Mixed Vegetable Stew): Use 250 gms of mixed vegetables (bittergourd, potato, colocasia, string beans, etc.) instead of potatoes. Add 2 petals chopped

cambodge after vegetables are tender, bring to boil, and continue as given.

Irachi Istoo (Meat Stew): Cook 500 gms cubed meat in a pressure cooker with 2 chopped onions, 8 slit green chillies, pepper, salt and ½ cup water for 30 minutes, and proceed as given, using 2 cups coconut milk.

Meen Istoo (Fish Stew): Use 250 gms of fish with 2 petals chopped cambodge. Cook over low heat for 10 minutes and continue as given.

URULAKIZHANGU PODIMAS
Spicy Mashed Potato

Serves: 4

2 medium-sized potatoes
2 tbsp oil
1 tsp mustard seeds
1 tsp husked black beans (urad dal)
1 medium-sized onion, chopped
8 green chillies, slit
5-cm piece ginger, chopped
1 stalk curry leaves
1 tsp turmeric powder
1 tsp salt

- Wash potatoes and boil in plenty of water till tender.
- Drain, peel and cut into 5-cm pieces.
- Heat oil in a pan and sprinkle in mustard seeds and dal. When mustard seeds start sputtering, add onion, green chillies, ginger and curry leaves, and fry till onion turns translucent.
- Sprinkle in turmeric and salt, and mix in potatoes and ¾ cup water.
- Cover pan and cook for 10 minutes over moderate heat.
- Open pan and mash potatoes.
- Serve with pathiri or porotta.

THENGAYUAM PULIYUM CHERTHA PODIMAS
Mashed Potato with Coconut and Tamarind

Serves: 4

6 medium-sized potatoes
2 medium-sized tomatoes, chopped
1 tsp salt

Ground to a fine paste:
½ medium-sized, fresh coconut, grated
6 dry red chillies, torn into pieces
A walnut-sized ball of seedless tamarind or 2-3 pieces
cambodge or unripe mango
¾ cup water

Tempering:
1½ tbsp oil
1 tsp mustard seeds
A pinch of asafoetida powder (hing)
A pinch of fenugreek seeds (methi)
1 stalk curry leaves

- Wash potatoes and boil in plenty of water till tender.
- Drain, peel, place in a pan and mash well.
- Mix in tomatoes, salt, coconut paste and 1½ cups water, and cook over high heat, stirring frequently, till it becomes semi-solid. Lower heat, simmer for 5 minutes more and remove from heat.
- Heat oil for tempering in a small pan and sprinkle in mustard seeds. When they start sputtering, add remaining ingredients and fry till fragrant.
- Pour contents of pan into potatoes, mix well and serve with rice, pathiri or porotta.

AVIAL
Mixed Vegetable Curry with Coconut and Curd

Serves: 8

Avial is one of the dishes that is always served at feasts. Since all the vegetables have to blend well, they must be cut evenly, usually about 5-cm long and 1-cm wide.

Because avial combines many vegetables, in colloquial Malayalam it means to mix or mess up!

4 drumsticks (surjan ki phalli)
50 gms string beans (lobia)
50 gms elephant foot yam (zimikand)
50 gms colocasia (arbi)
2 unripe plantains
50 gms cucumber
1½ tsp salt
2 tbsp curd (not too sour), whisked
1 stalk curry leaves
1½ tbsp coconut oil

Ground to a coarse paste:
1 medium-sized, fresh coconut, grated
6 shallots, chopped
10 green chillies, chopped
1 stalk curry leaves
A pinch of cumin powder
½ tsp turmeric powder

- Peel drumsticks, string and trim beans, and cut into 5-cm long pieces. Peel remaining vegetables and cut into 5-cm long and 1-cm wide strips.
- Place vegetables in a pan with salt and 1½ cups water, and cook over high heat for 20 minutes till tender.

- Stir in curd and coconut paste, and cook for 2 minutes.
- Add curry leaves and oil. Mix well and serve.

Variations: Use tamarind or unripe mango instead of curd. In some parts of Kerala, a piece of bittergourd is also added. This lends a certain piquancy to the dish.

THENGAPAL CHERTHA CHEERA KARI
Amaranthus and Coconut Milk Curry

Serves: 8

150 gms amaranthus (cholai)
1½ tbsp oil
1 tsp mustard seeds
1 medium-sized onion, chopped
3-cm piece ginger, chopped
10 green chillies, chopped
1 stalk curry leaves
1 tsp black pepper powder
1 tsp salt
1 cup coconut milk (1st extract; see p. 20)

- Wash amaranthus thoroughly and chop fine.
- Heat oil in a pan and sprinkle in mustard seeds. When they start sputtering, add onion, ginger, green chillies and curry leaves, and fry till onion turns translucent.
- Mix in amaranthus, pepper and salt, cover pan and cook over low heat for 5 minutes till amaranthus is tender.
- Pour in coconut milk and cook for 2 minutes longer.

KUMBALANGA OLAN
Ashgourd Curry with Cowpeas and Coconut Milk

Serves: 8

This olan is one of the eight dishes served at feasts.

½ cup red cowpeas (lobia)
200 gms ashgourd (petha)
6 green chillies, slit
1 tsp salt
1 + 1 stalks curry leaves
1 cup coconut milk (1st extract; see p. 20)
2½ tbsp oil

- Wash cowpeas and soak overnight in water.
- Drain, rinse, and place in a pressure cooker with ¾ cup water. Cook under pressure for 10-15 minutes.
- Peel ashgourd and cut into 3-cm cubes.
- Put ashgourd, green chillies, salt and 1 stalk curry leaves in a pan with ¾ cup water and cook over high heat for 30 minutes till tender.
- Mash ashgourd lightly, mix in cowpeas and coconut milk, and simmer for 2 minutes.
- Stir in oil and 1 stalk curry leaves, mix well and serve.

Variations: While cowpeas remain a constant, cucumber or unripe papaya can be substituted for ashgourd. However in a feast ashgourd is considered essential.

Mathanga Olan (Pumpkin Curry with Coconut Milk): Omit cowpeas. Cook 500 gms red pumpkin, cut into 3-cm cubes for 15-20 minutes, taking care not to break the pieces. Here coconut oil adds to the flavour.

MANGA PACHADI
Unripe Mango Curry with Curd and Coconut

Serves: 4

Manga pachadi is one of the eight dishes served at feasts.

100 gms unripe mangoes (not too sour)
1 tsp salt
¾ cup curd (not too sour), whisked

Ground to a fine paste:
½ medium-sized, fresh coconut, grated
4 shallots, chopped
6 green chillies, chopped
1 tsp mustard seeds
A pinch of cumin powder
¾ cup water

Tempering:
1½ tbsp oil
2 stalks curry leaves

- Peel mangoes and cut into 1-cm cubes.
- Place mangoes in a pan with salt and ¾ cup water, and cook over high heat for about 10 minutes.
- Mix curd with coconut paste and stir into mangoes. Bring to boil and remove pan from heat immediately.
- Heat oil for tempering in a small pan, add curry leaves and fry for a moment.
- Pour contents of pan into pachadi, mix well and serve.

PAZHAVUM PACHAKARIYUM CHERTHA PACHADI
Fruit and Vegetable Curry with Curd and Coconut

Serves: 8

It is only in the last four decades that tomatoes and grapes
have become widely available in Kerala. So these additions
to the traditional sweet pachadi is a recent development.
The pineapple and mango should not be completely ripe.

750 gms pineapple
2 medium-sized table mangoes
3 medium-sized tomatoes
½ tsp turmeric powder
1 tsp red chilli powder
1 tsp salt
¾ cup curd (not sour), whisked
250 gms seedless black grapes
1 tsp sugar

Ground to a fine paste:
½ medium-sized, fresh coconut, grated
¾ cup water

Ground to a fine paste:
4 green chillies, chopped
½ tsp mustard seeds
2 tbsp water

Tempering:
2 tsp oil
½ tsp mustard seeds
1 tsp husked Bengal gram (chana dal)
1 stalk curry leaves

- Peel pineapple and mangoes. Cut pineapples, mangoes and tomatoes into 1-cm cubes and place in a pan.
- Add spice powders, salt and 5 tbsp water, and mix well.
- Place pan over high heat and cook for about 10 minutes, stirring occasionally.
- Mix curd with coconut and chilli pastes, and stir into pan.
- Bring to boil, add grapes and remove from heat immediately.
- Heat oil for tempering in a small pan and sprinkle in mustard seeds. When they start sputtering, add dal and fry till dal turns red. Add curry leaves and fry for a moment longer.
- Pour contents of pan into curry, stir in sugar and serve.

Variation:

Mampazha Pachadi (Ripe Mango Curry with Coconut): Use 500 gms small table mangoes cut into small pieces, with skin, instead of the fruits used in the recipe above. Increase chilli powder to 2 tsp and turmeric powder to 1 tsp. Omit curd and sugar, and dal and curry leaves in the tempering. Cook mangoes in the same way, adding jaggery to taste if mangoes are not sweet enough.

PAVAKKA PACHADI
Sautéed Bittergourd Curry with Curd and Coconut

Serves: 4

150 gms bittergourds (karela)
1 tbsp oil
1 cup curd (not sour), whisked
1 tsp salt

Ground to a very fine paste:
½ medium-sized, fresh coconut, grated
6 green chillies, chopped
½ tsp mustard seeds
¾ cup water

Tempering:

1 tbsp oil
½ tsp mustard seeds

- Wash bittergourds, remove seeds and chop.
- Heat oil in a pan, add bittergourds, sauté over moderate heat till brown and set aside.
- Mix curd with coconut paste in a pan and set aside.
- Heat oil for tempering in a small pan and sprinkle in mustard seeds. When they start sputtering, pour contents of pan into coconut-curd mixture.
- Stir in salt and cook over moderate heat for about 5 minutes.
- Add bittergourds. Mix well and remove from heat.
- Allow to cool and thicken slightly, and serve.

Variations: Okra (bhindi), shallot, aubergine (baingan), cucumber, ripe pineapple or ripe plantain can be used instead of bittergourd.

PAVAKKA KICHADI
Bittergourd Curry with Curd and Coconut

Serves: 4

This is another of the ettukoottam kari.

The differences between a pachadi and a kichadi are subtle in that the sequence of steps is different, and sometimes, the number of ingredients varies.

200 gms bittergourds (karela)
3 tsp oil
½ tsp mustard seeds
1 tsp husked Bengal gram (chana dal)
1 stalk curry leaves
3 green chillies, chopped
¾ cup curd (not sour), whisked
1 tsp salt

Ground to a fine paste:
½ medium-sized, fresh coconut, grated
3 green chillies, chopped
½ tsp mustard seeds
¾ cup water

- Wash bittergourds, remove seeds and chop.
- Heat oil in a pan and sprinkle in mustard seeds. When they start sputtering, add gram and fry till it turns red. Stir in curry leaves, green chillies and bittergourds, and sauté till bittergourds turn brown.
- Mix curd with salt and coconut paste, add to pan, mix well and cook for 5 minutes more.

Variations: Okra (bhindi), carrot, beetroot or unripe mango can be substituted for bittergourd.

PULINKARI
Sour Vegetable Curry

Serves: 8

This is a regular dish on many household menus.

200 gms red pumpkin (kaddu)
100 gms cucumber
1 tsp salt
A walnut-sized ball of seedless tamarind soaked in 2 tbsp water

Coconut-spice paste:
10 dry red chillies, torn into pieces
1 tsp fenugreek seeds (methi)
1 medium-sized, fresh coconut, grated (optional)

Tempering:
1 tbsp oil
1 tsp mustard seeds

- Dry roast red chillies and fenugreek seeds for coconut-spice paste individually in a pan over moderate heat.
- Brown coconut (if used) in a frying pan over high heat. Cool, mix all ingredients and grind coarsely.
- Peel and cut vegetables into 3-cm cubes.
- Place vegetables in a pan with salt and 1½ cups water, and cook over high heat for 20 minutes till tender.
- Extract tamarind pulp and strain into pan. Stir in coconut-spice paste, bring to boil and remove from heat immediately.
- Heat oil for tempering in a small pan and sprinkle in mustard seeds. When they start sputtering, pour contents of pan into curry, mix well and serve.

PAVAKKA THEEYAL
Bittergourd Curry with Fried Coconut

Serves: 6

In a theeyal, the spices and coconut are fried and ground to a fine paste before being cooked.

100 gms bittergourds (karela)
½ tbsp oil
8 shallots, chopped
3 green chillies, slit
A walnut-sized ball of seedless tamarind soaked in 2 tsp water
1 tsp salt

Coconut-spice paste:
½ tbsp oil
1 medium-sized, fresh coconut, grated
4 shallots, chopped
10 dry red chillies, torn into pieces
6 black peppercorns
1 stalk curry leaves
1 tsp coriander powder
½ tsp turmeric powder

Tempering:
1 tbsp oil
1 tsp mustard seeds
2 dry red chillies, torn into pieces
3 shallots, chopped
1 stalk curry leaves

- Heat oil for coconut-spice paste in a frying pan.
- Add all ingredients except spice powders, and fry, stirring constantly, till coconut turns brown.
- Remove from heat, stir in coriander powder, allow to

cool and mix in turmeric powder.
- Grind to a fine paste with 1½ cups water.
- Wash bittergourds, remove seeds, cut into 3-cm pieces and set aside.
- Heat ½ tbsp oil in a pan, add bittergourds, shallots and green chillies, and sauté till bittergourds turn brown.
- Extract tamarind pulp and strain into pan.
- Stir in coconut-spice paste, salt and 1¼ cups water. Raise heat, boil for 10 minutes and remove from heat.
- Heat oil for tempering in a small pan and sprinkle in mustard seeds. When they start sputtering, toss in red chillies and fry for a few moments till fragrant, shaking the pan occasionally. Add remaining ingredients and fry till shallots turn brown.
- Pour contents of pan into curry, mix well and serve.

Variation: Theeyal can also be made with shallots, okra (bhindi) or French beans instead of bittergourd.

MURINGAKAYUM MANGAYUM CHERTHA PACHHA THEEYAL

Drumstick and Unripe Mango Curry with Coconut

Serves: 8

Pachha means green. Here it signifies the fact that spices, coconut and vegetables are cooked without frying, as is the norm for a theeyal.

4 drumsticks (surjan ki phalli)
1 unripe mango
5 shallots, chopped
4 green chillies, slit
2 tsp red chilli powder
1 tsp coriander powder
½ tsp turmeric powder
1 tsp salt

Ground to a very fine paste:
1 medium-sized, fresh coconut, grated
3 shallots, chopped
1 tsp cumin seeds
1½ cups water

Tempering:
2 tbsp oil
1 tsp mustard seeds
2 shallots, chopped
1 stalk curry leaves

- Peel and cut drumstick into 7-cm pieces. Peel and cut mango into 1-cm cubes.
- Put drumsticks, mango, shallots, green chillies, spice powders and salt in a pan. Mix well and add 1½ cups water.

- Place pan over high heat and cook for for 5-10 minutes till drumsticks are tender. Add a little more water if it tends to get dry.
- Add coconut paste and mix well. Bring to boil and remove from heat immediately.
- Heat oil for tempering in a small pan and sprinkle in mustard seeds. When they start sputtering, add remaining ingredients and fry till shallots turn brown.
- Pour contents of pan into curry, mix well and serve.

Variation: A handful of cleaned, sliced jackfruit seeds added with the drumsticks and mango enhances the taste.

URULAKIZHANGU MAPAS
Potato Curry with Coconut Milk

Serves: 4

A Christian dish, mapas is a curry with coconut milk and fine spices. This recipe is a vegetarian version of what is essentially a non-vegetarian dish.

2 medium-sized potatoes
1 medium-sized onion, chopped
2 green chillies, slit
3-cm piece ginger, chopped
1 tsp red chilli powder
1 tsp coriander powder
1 tsp turmeric powder
1 tsp salt
1 cup coconut milk (1st extract; see p. 20)

Coarsely ground:

1 clove garlic, chopped
3-cm stick cinnamon, broken into pieces
2 cloves
A pinch of fennel seeds (badi saunf)
3 black peppercorns

Tempering:

2 tbsp oil
1 tsp mustard seeds
2 shallots, chopped
1 stalk curry leaves

- Peel potatoes and cut into 5-cm pieces.
- Mix potatoes and ground spices in a pan. Add onion, green chillies, ginger, spice powders, salt and ¾ cup water, and mix well.
- Cover pan and cook over high heat for about 15 minutes, till potatoes are tender. Gently break potatoes into smaller pieces with a ladle.
- Add coconut milk, simmer for about 2 minutes and remove pan from heat.
- Heat oil for tempering in a small pan and sprinkle in mustard seeds. When they start sputtering, add remaining ingredients and fry till shallots turn brown.
- Pour contents of pan into curry, mix well and serve with rice, puttu, appam or idiappam.

Variations: Vegetable mapas can also be made with sautéed okra (bhindi) or cabbage.

INJIUM THAIRUM CHERTHA PAVAKKA KARI
Bittergourd Curry with Ginger and Curd

Serves: 4

100 gms bittergourds (karela)
1½ tbsp oil
½ tsp mustard seeds
2 shallots, chopped
1 stalk curry leaves
1 tsp salt
1 cup curd (not sour), whisked

Ground to a fine paste:
½ medium-sized, fresh coconut, grated
2 shallots, chopped
6 green chillies, chopped
5-cm piece ginger, chopped
1 stalk curry leaves
½ tsp mustard seeds
¾ cup water

- Wash bittergourds, remove seeds and chop.
- Heat oil in a pan and sprinkle in mustard seeds. When they start sputtering, add shallots and curry leaves, and fry till shallots turn brown.
- Add bittergourds and sauté for about 5 minutes.
- Sprinkle in salt and scant ½ cup water, mix well, cover pan and cook over low heat for 10 minutes till bittergourds are tender.
- Mix in curd and coconut paste, heat through and serve.

Variations: Instead of bittergourd, okra (bhindi), cucumber or unripe papaya can be used.

KAPPA PUZHUKKU
Tapioca Potage

Serves: 8

This is the all-time favourite in the toddy shops of Kerala. It is usually served with a spicy fish curry, but can also be eaten as a meal in itself with a pungent coconut chutney.

500 gms tapioca
1 tsp salt

Ground to a coarse paste:
½ medium-sized, fresh coconut, grated
5 shallots, chopped
10 dry red chillies, torn into pieces
A pinch of cumin powder
½ tsp turmeric powder

Tempering:
1½ tbsp oil
1 tsp mustard seeds
1 shallot, chopped
1 stalk curry leaves

- Peel, wash and cut tapioca into 1-cm pieces.
- Place in a pan with enough water to cover, and boil over high heat for 30 minutes till cooked.
- Drain, stir in salt and mash lightly.
- Return pan to low heat, mix in coconut paste and cook for 5 minutes, stirring occasionally.
- Heat oil for tempering in a small pan and sprinkle in mustard seeds. When they start sputtering, add remaining ingredients and fry till shallot turns brown. Pour contents of pan into puzhukku, mix well and serve.

THIRUVATHIRA PUZHUKKU
Vegetable Potage

Serves: 8

This dish is made especially on Thiruvathira, a festival in December/January, celebrating the victory of Rathi (the goddess of desire) gaining immortality for her husband Kamadeva (the god of love), who was annihilated by Shiva. The festival is celebrated exclusively by women.

The majority of the vegetables used in this dish significantly are tubers that grow beneath the ground or the womb of the earth.

¼ cup red cowpeas (lobia)
¼ cup horsegram (kulthi ka dal)
50 gms colocasia (arbi)
50 gms yam (chupri aloo)
50 gms unripe plantain
50 gms sweet potato
50 gms elephant foot yam (zimikand)
50 gms Malabar catmint (koorka)
1 tsp salt

Ground to a coarse paste:
1 medium-sized, fresh coconut, grated
6 shallots, chopped
10 dry red chillies, torn into pieces
A pinch of cumin seeds
½ tsp turmeric powder

Tempering:
2 tbsp oil
1 stalk curry leaves

- Wash cowpeas and horsegram and soak overnight in water.
- Drain, rinse, place in a pan with 3¼ cups fresh water and cook over high heat for 30 minutes till half-cooked.
- Peel, clean and cut vegetables into 1-cm pieces.
- Add vegetables to pan and cook for 30 minutes till tender.
- Stir in salt and coconut paste, and remove from heat.
- Heat oil for tempering in a small pan and fry curry leaves for a few moments.
- Pour contents of pan into puzhukku, mix well and serve.

PAVAKA VARATHATHU
Deep-fried Bittergourd

Serves: 8

500 gms bittergourds (karela)
1 tbsp red chilli powder
1 tsp turmeric powder
¼ fresh coconut, chopped
2 tsp salt
1 cup oil

- Wash bittergourds, slit, remove seeds and slice fine.
- Mix with spice powders, coconut and salt and set aside for an hour.
- Heat oil in a kadhai or wok and deep fry bittergourds till crisp.

KUMBALANGA PULISSERI
Ashgourd Curry with Buttermilk

Serves: 8

This curry is especially popular in south Kerala where it is also served at feasts.

500 gms ashgourd (petha)
1 tsp turmeric powder
2½ cups sour buttermilk (chhaas)
1 tsp salt
1 stalk curry leaves

Ground to a fine paste:
½ medium-sized, fresh coconut, grated
10 green chillies, chopped
A pinch of cumin seeds
1 tsp parboiled rice (soaked in water for 15 minutes and drained)
¾ cup water

Tempering:
2 tbsp oil
½ tsp mustard seeds
3 dry red chillies, torn into pieces
½ tsp fenugreek seeds (methi)

- Peel, clean and cut ashgourd into 5-cm cubes.
- Combine ashgourd, turmeric and ¾ cup water in a pan, place over high heat and boil for 15-20 minutes till tender.
- Mix coconut paste with buttermilk and stir it in with salt. Bring to boil, add curry leaves and remove from heat immediately.
- Heat oil for tempering in a small pan and sprinkle in

mustard seeds. When they start sputtering, toss in remaining ingredients and fry for a few moments till fragrant, shaking the pan occasionally.
- Pour contents of pan into curry, mix well and serve.

YOGYARATHNA
Mixed Vegetable Curry with Coconut Milk

Serves: 8

A Konkani dish.

50 gms string beans (lobia)
50 gms red pumpkin (kaddu)
50 gms ashgourd (petha)
1 small potato
50 gms colocasia (arbi)
2½ tbsp split cashewnuts
8 green chillies, slit
1 tsp salt
1 cup coconut milk (2nd extract; see p. 20)
½ cup coconut milk (1st extract)
1½ tbsp coconut oil
A pinch of asafoetida powder (hing)

- Trim and string beans, and cut into 3-cm pieces. Peel and cut remaining vegetables into thin, 3-cm slices.
- Place vegetables, cashewnuts, green chillies, salt and second extract of coconut milk in a pan, and cook over high heat till vegetables are tender.
- Lower heat, stir in first extract of coconut milk, and simmer for 2 minutes.
- Mix in oil and asafoetida powder and serve.

THENGA CHERTHA ULLI SAMBAR
Shallot and Coconut Sambar

Serves: 8

Though sambar is a must at feasts, it is not a Malayali dish. However, this variation with coconut is specific to Kerala. It is rarely served at feasts where the preference is for vegetable sambar.

1¼ cups pigeon peas (arhar/toover dal)
500 gms shallots, peeled and kept whole
5 green chillies, slit
A lime-sized ball of seedless tamarind soaked in 5 tbsp water
1 sprig coriander leaves, chopped

Coconut-spice paste:
½ medium-sized, fresh coconut, grated
50 gms sambar powder (see p. 33)
1 tsp turmeric powder
1 tsp red chilli powder
1 tsp asafoetida powder (hing)
2 tsp salt

Tempering:
2 tbsp coconut oil
1 tsp mustard seeds
1 tsp husked black beans (urad dal)
2 dry red chillies, torn into pieces
2 stalks curry leaves

- Place coconut for the coconut-spice paste in a frying pan over low heat, and dry-roast, stirring constantly, till it turns brown. Cool and grind to a fine paste with ¾ cup water. Mix in spice powders and salt.
- Wash dal and place in a pan with shallots, green chillies

68   *The Essential Kerala Cookbook*

and 1½ cups water. Cook over high heat for 20 minutes till dal is tender.

- Mash lightly and add coconut-spice paste.
- Extract tamarind pulp, strain into pan and mix well.
- Bring to boil, remove from heat immediately and add coriander leaves.
- Heat oil for tempering in a small pan and sprinkle in mustard seeds. When they start sputtering, toss in dal and red chillies, and fry for a few moments till fragrant, shaking the pan occasionally. Add curry leaves and fry for a moment longer.
- Pour contents of pan into sambar, mix well and serve.

THUVARAPARIPPU KARI
Spicy Pigeon Pea Curry

Serves: 4

½ cup pigeon peas (arhar/toover dal)
A pinch of turmeric powder
¼ tsp red chilli powder
4 green chillies, slit
1 tsp salt

Ground to a fine paste:
½ medium-sized, fresh coconut, grated
3 shallots, chopped
A pinch of cumin seeds
¾ cup water

Tempering:
1½ tbsp oil
1 tsp mustard seeds
2 dry red chillies, torn into pieces
1 stalk curry leaves

- Wash dal, place in a pan with spice powders and ¾ cup water, and cook over high heat for 20 minutes.
- Add green chillies and salt, and bring to boil.
- Stir in coconut paste, bring to boil again and remove from heat immediately.
- Heat oil for tempering in a small pan and sprinkle in mustard seeds. When they start sputtering, toss in red chillies and fry for a few moments till fragrant, shaking the pan occasionally. Add curry leaves, and fry for a moment longer.
- Pour contents of pan into curry, mix well and serve.

MOLOSHYAM
Spicy Pigeon Pea Curry with Vegetables

Serves: 4

This is a popular dish on most household menus. It is also called moleeshyam in some parts of Kerala.

4 drumsticks (surjan ki phalli)
½ cup pigeon peas (arhar/toover dal)
10 shallots, peeled and kept whole
1 tsp turmeric powder
20 black peppercorns, coarsely ground
1 tsp salt
15 curry leaves

Ground to a fine paste:
½ medium-sized, fresh coconut, grated
A pinch of cumin seeds
¾ cup water

Tempering:
2 tbsp oil
½ tsp mustard seeds
3 dry red chillies, torn into pieces
4 shallots, chopped
5 curry leaves

- Peel and cut drumsticks into 5-cm long pieces.
- Wash dal, place in a pan with ¾ cup water over high heat and boil for 20 minutes.
- Mix in drumsticks, shallots, spice powders and salt, and cook for about 10 minutes till drumsticks are tender.
- Stir in coconut paste and bring to boil. Add curry leaves

and remove from heat immediately.
- Heat oil for tempering in a small pan and sprinkle in mustard seeds. When they start sputtering, toss in red chillies and fry for a few moments till fragrant, shaking the pan occasionally. Add shallots and curry leaves, and fry till shallots turn brown.
- Pour contents of pan into curry, mix well and serve.

Variation: Moloshyam can be made without coconut. Just powder cumin seeds coarsely, and add when drumsticks are cooked.

KADALA KARI
Whole Bengal Gram Curry

Serves: 8

1½ cups whole Bengal gram (kala chana)
2 tbsp oil
½ tsp mustard seeds
2 medium-sized onions, chopped
2 green chillies, chopped
3-cm piece ginger, chopped
1 stalk curry leaves
1 tsp salt

Mixed together:

2 tsp red chilli powder
1 tsp coriander powder
½ tsp cumin powder
½ tsp turmeric powder
½ tsp black pepper powder
2 cloves, powdered
½ tsp powdered cinnamon
2 tsp water

Ground to a fine paste:
½ medium-sized, fresh coconut, grated
¾ cup water

- Wash gram and soak overnight in water. Drain, rinse and place in a pressure cooker with ¾ cup water, and cook under pressure for 30 minutes.
- Heat oil in a pan and sprinkle in mustard seeds. When they start sputtering, add onions and fry till translucent.
- Mix in green chillies, ginger and curry leaves, and fry

73

for 2 minutes, stirring occasionally.
- Stir in spice paste and fry for a minute longer.
- Add salt, ⅓ cup water and dal with its gravy. Raise heat and boil for 5 minutes.
- Add coconut paste and cook for 2 minutes, stirring constantly.
- This curry is traditionally served with puttu and an accompaniment of pappadum.

Variations: Fry small pieces of coconut along with the onions and use instead of the coconut paste.

Pachakari Chertha Kadala Kari (Whole Bengal Gram Curry with Vegetables): Reduce Bengal gram to ½ cup and pressure-cook for 30 minutes. Add 100 gms each of elephant foot yam (zimikand) and unripe plantain, cut into 3-cm pieces. Pressure-cook for 5 minutes more and continue as given.

MURINGAYILA KARI
Drumstick Leaf Curry

Serves: 4

Dishes made with the leaves of drumsticks, ashgourd, colocasia, cowpeas, red pumpkin, etc., play a prominent role in household menus after the fury of the monsoon subsides. They are chosen for their taste and medicinal values. This recipe is from the Muslim community.

100 gms drumstick leaves
2 tbsp oil
1 tsp mustard seeds
1 stalk curry leaves
½ tsp red chilli powder
½ tsp turmeric powder
½ tsp salt

Ground to a fine paste:
½ medium-sized, fresh coconut, grated
3 shallots, chopped
A pinch of cumin seeds
¾ cup water

- Clean and wash drumstick leaves, and drain well.
- Heat oil in a pan and sprinkle in mustard seeds. When they start sputtering, add curry leaves and spice powders, and fry over low heat for 30 seconds, stirring constantly.
- Add salt and drumstick leaves, and fry over moderate heat for 10 minutes, stirring occasionally.
- Mix in coconut paste and ¾ cup water, and bring to boil. Remove from heat immediately and serve with rice or pathiri.

URULAKIZHANGU KARI
Spicy Potato Curry

Serves: 8

A Christian dish.

2 medium-sized potatoes
2 tbsp oil
1 tsp mustard seeds
¼ medium-sized, fresh coconut, chopped into 1-cm pieces
2 shallots, chopped
3-cm piece ginger, chopped
1 stalk curry leaves
1 tsp salt
1 medium-sized onion, sliced

Ground to a fine paste:
2 shallots, chopped
1 clove garlic, chopped
2 tsp red chilli powder
2 tsp coriander powder
4 black peppercorns
3-cm stick cinnamon, broken into pieces
1 clove
A pinch of fennel seeds (badi saunf)
1 tsp turmeric powder
4 tsp water

- Peel potatoes and cut into 3-cm cubes.
- Heat oil in a pan and sprinkle in mustard seeds. When they start sputtering, add coconut, shallots, ginger and curry leaves, and fry, stirring constantly, till coconut turns brown. Stir in salt, spice paste, and 1½ cups water, and bring to boil.
- Mix in potatoes and onion, cover pan and cook over

The Essential Kerala Cookbook

high heat for about 20 minutes till tender.
- Break potatoes gently with the back of a ladle to thicken gravy.

Variation: Breadfruit can be substituted for potato.

MUTTAKOOS THORAN
Stir-fried Cabbage with Coconut

Serves: 8

In a thoran, vegetables are always cut small and cooked with grated, ground or chopped coconut.

250 gms cabbage
2 tbsp coconut oil
1 tsp mustard seeds
1 medium-sized onion, chopped
6 green chillies, slit
1 stalk curry leaves
1 tsp salt
½ medium-sized, fresh coconut, grated

- Chop cabbage very fine.
- Heat oil in a pan and sprinkle in mustard seeds. When they start sputtering, add onion, green chillies and curry leaves, and fry till onion turns translucent.
- Mix in cabbage and salt. Press down with a spatula, cover pan and cook for 5 minutes over low heat.
- Open pan, add coconut and stir-fry till completely dry.

Variations: Bittergourd, carrot, capsicum or okra (bhindi) can be used instead of cabbage. Add 2 chopped petals of cambodge with bittergourd.

KUDAPPAN THORAN
Stir-fried Banana Flower with Coconut

Serves: 4

500 gms banana flower
1 tbsp + 1 tbsp coconut oil
1 tsp mustard seeds
2 tsp parboiled rice
2 shallots, chopped
1 stalk curry leaves
1 tsp salt

Ground to a coarse paste:
½ medium-sized, fresh coconut, grated
2 shallots, chopped
6 dry red chillies, torn into pieces
A pinch of cumin seeds
½ tsp turmeric powder

- Remove and discard all the outer petals of banana flower till the white inner petal is seen.
- Chop very fine and mix in 1 tbsp oil. Knead gently till it loses its stickiness and becomes soft.
- Heat 1 tbsp oil in a pan and sprinkle in mustard seeds and rice. When mustard seeds start sputtering, add shallots and curry leaves, and fry till shallots turn brown.
- Stir in coconut paste and salt, and fry, stirring frequently, for 2 minutes.
- Add banana flower. Mix well and press down well with a spatula. Cover pan and cook over low heat for 10 minutes.

- Open pan and stir-fry for 5 minutes longer.

Variation: The core of the banana trunk chopped fine can also be cooked in this manner.

CHAKKAKURU THORAN
Stir-fried Jackfruit Seeds with Coconut

Serves: 4

250 gms jackfruit seeds
1½ tbsp coconut oil
1 tsp mustard seeds
1 shallot, chopped
1 stalk curry leaves
1 tsp salt

Ground to a fine paste:
½ medium-sized, fresh coconut, grated
5 shallots, chopped
6 green chillies, chopped
A pinch of cumin seeds
½ tsp turmeric powder

- Peel jackfruit seeds. Clean and cut into 1-cm pieces.
- Heat oil in a pan and sprinkle in mustard seeds. When they start sputtering, add shallot and curry leaves, and fry till shallot turns brown.
- Stir in coconut paste and fry, stirring frequently, for 2 minutes.
- Mix in jackfruit seeds, salt and ¾ cup water. Cover pan and cook over low heat for 15 minutes.
- Open pan and stir-fry till dry.

IDICHAKKA THORAN
Stir-fried Tender Jackfruit with Coconut

Serves: 8

500 gms tender jackfruit
1 tsp salt
2 tbsp coconut oil
1 tsp mustard seeds
2 shallots, chopped
1 stalk curry leaves

Ground to a coarse paste:
1 medium-sized, fresh coconut, grated
3 shallots, chopped
10 dry red chillies, torn into pieces
½ tsp turmeric powder
A pinch of cumin seeds

- Remove outer part of jackfruit and inner fibres, and cut fruit into large pieces along with any unripe seeds.
- Place in a pressure cooker with salt and ¾ cup water and cook under pressure for 10 minutes.
- Remove from heat, allow to cool and mash well.
- Heat oil in a pan and sprinkle in mustard seeds. When they start sputtering, add shallots and curry leaves, and fry till shallots turn brown.
- Add coconut paste and jackfruit, and stir-fry till dry.

Variation: **Vazhuthananga Thoran (Stir-fried Aubergine with Coconut)**: Use 250 gms aubergine (baingan) instead of jackfruit. Slice and soak in water with 1 tsp salt for 20 minutes. Drain, rinse and dry. Add to pan with coconut paste and 1 tsp salt, and stir-fry till dry.

MURINGAYILA THORAN
Stir-fried Drumstick Leaves with Coconut

Serves: 4

250 gms drumstick leaves
1½ tbsp coconut oil
1 tsp mustard seeds
1 tsp rice
2 shallots, chopped
1 tsp salt

Ground to a coarse paste:
½ medium-sized, fresh coconut, grated
4 shallots, chopped
6 dry red chillies, torn into pieces
A pinch of cumin seeds
½ tsp turmeric powder

- Clean and wash drumstick leaves and drain.
- Heat oil in a pan and sprinkle in mustard seeds and rice. When mustard seeds start sputtering, add shallots and fry till brown.
- Stir in coconut paste and fry for 2 minutes. Mix in drumstick leaves and salt. Press down with a spatula, cover pan and cook over low heat for a minute.
- Open pan and stir-fry till dry.

Variations: Drumstick flowers can be used instead of the leaves.

Muringakai Thoran (Stir-fried Drumsticks with Coconut):
Scrape out the inner portion of 10 drumsticks and use instead of leaves. Use 4 green chillies instead of red. Omit rice and fry 1 stalk curry leaves with shallots.

81

KAYA MEZHUKKUPURATTI
Stir-Fried Unripe Plantain

Serves: 6

In a mezhukkupuratti (that which is coated in oil), the vegetables are cut small and the cooking is over low heat with brisk stirring. A cheenachatti (kadhai/wok) or a heavy-based frying pan is ideal for preparing this dish as it minimises the use of water. Fine spices (cloves, etc.) and coconut are avoided. A mezhukkupuratti is not served at feasts.

250 gms unripe plantain
2 tbsp oil
1 tsp mustard seeds
10 shallots, chopped
6 green chillies, slit
1 stalk curry leaves
1 tsp black pepper powder
½ tsp turmeric powder
1 tsp salt

- Peel plantain and cut into thin, 3-cm long slices.
- Heat oil in a kadhai and sprinkle in mustard seeds. When they start sputtering, add shallots, green chillies and curry leaves, and fry till shallots turn brown.
- Mix in plantain, spice powders and salt, cover kadhai and cook over low heat for 10 minutes.
- Open pan, stir-fry till dry and serve.

Variations: Instead of unripe plantain, Malabar catmint (koorka), potato, okra (bhindi), string beans (lobia), jackfruit seeds or snakegourd (chirchinda) can be used.

CAULIFLOWER MEZHUKKUPURATTI
Stir-Fried Cauliflower

Serves: 4

250 gms cauliflower
1 tsp turmeric powder
1 tsp + 1 tsp salt
1½ tbsp oil
1 tsp mustard seeds
4 green chillies, slit
1 stalk curry leaves

- Cut cauliflower into small florets and wash well.
- Place 2½ cups water in a pan with turmeric and 1 tsp salt, and bring to boil.
- Remove pan from heat and immerse cauliflower in it for 5 minutes. Drain and dry cauliflower.
- Heat oil in a kadhai and sprinkle in mustard seeds. When they start sputtering, add green chillies, curry leaves and 1 tsp salt, and fry for 2 minutes.
- Mix in cauliflower and stir-fry till completely dry.

83

CHEMBU MEZHUKKUPURATTI
Stir-Fried Colocasia

Serves: 4

150 gms colocasia (arbi)
2 tbsp oil
1 tsp mustard seeds
6 shallots, chopped
1 stalk curry leaves
1 tsp red chilli powder
½ tsp turmeric powder
½ tsp black pepper powder
1 tsp salt

- Peel colocasia, wash and cut into thin, 3-cm long slices.
- Heat oil in a kadhai and sprinkle in mustard seeds. When they start sputtering, add shallots and curry leaves, and fry till shallots turn brown.
- Sprinkle in spice powders and salt, and stir in colocasia.
- Pour in ½ cup water, cover kadhai and cook over low heat for 15 minutes.
- Open kadhai and stir-fry till dry.

Variations: Elephant foot yam (zimikand) and green plantain, together or individually can be substituted for colocasia.

Thenga Chertha Chakkakuru Mezhukkupuratti (Stir-fried Jackfruit Seeds with Coconut): Use 250 gms jackfruit seeds, peeled, cleaned and cut into 1-cm pieces instead of the colocasia. Use ½ cup chopped fresh coconut instead of the shallots, fry till brown and continue as given.

84   *The Essential Kerala Cookbook*

MURINGAKAYA MEZHUKKUPURATTI
Stir-fried Drumsticks

Serves: 4

10 drumsticks (surjan ki phalli)
2 tbsp oil
1 tsp mustard seeds
1 tsp red chilli powder
½ tsp turmeric powder
1 tsp salt

- Peel and cut drumstick into 7-cm pieces.
- Heat oil in a kadhai and sprinkle in mustard seeds. When they start sputtering, add spice powders and salt. Mix in drumsticks, cover kadhai and cook over low heat for 10 minutes.
- Open pan and stir-fry till dry.

Meat, poultry and eggs

Malayali non-vegetarian cuisine, as we know it today, is based on the culinary traditions of the Christian and Muslim communities. There are five main methods used extensively, particularly in Syrian Christian cooking, for both meat and poultry:

- Varutharachathu where spices and grated coconut are fried, and then ground before being added to the pan
- Varatiathu (also called ularthiathu) in which meat and spices are cooked together to the point that very little gravy remains
- Varathathu or deep frying with or without a coating of spices
- Peralen in which the meat or poultry is prepared with a coating of gravy
- Mapas where the gravy is made with spices and coconut milk.

Muslim non-vegetarian cuisine is notable for its use of curd, cashewnuts and poppy seeds.

In Malayalam irachi means meat of any type. A prefix (aadu for goat, maadu for beef, panni for pig, pothu for buffalo, kozhi for chicken and tharavu for duck), before the word indicates the specific meat. However, in colloquial Malayalam irachi commonly refers to the meat of goat, cow or buffalo.

IRACHI VARUTHARACHATHU
Meat Cooked with Ground Coconut

Serves: 4

A Christian dish.

500 gms mutton or beef
2 medium-sized onions, sliced
3 medium-sized tomatoes, quartered
3 green chillies, slit
5-cm piece ginger, chopped
1 tsp salt

Coconut-spice paste:

1 tbsp oil
½ medium-sized, fresh coconut, grated
6 shallots, chopped
12 dry red chillies, torn into pieces
1 stalk curry leaves
2 tsp coriander powder
2 cloves garlic, chopped
1 tsp black pepper powder
5-cm stick cinnamon, broken into pieces
3 cloves
1 tsp fennel seeds (badi saunf)
1 tsp turmeric powder

Tempering:

1 tbsp oil
1 tsp mustard seeds
4 shallots, chopped
1 stalk curry leaves

• Heat oil for coconut-spice paste in a frying pan. Add coconut, shallots, red chillies and curry leaves, and

fry, stirring constantly, till coconut turns brown. Mix in coriander powder and remove from heat.
- Allow to cool, mix with remaining ingredients for paste and grind with ¾ cup water to a fine paste.
- Wash meat, drain and cut into 3-cm pieces.
- Place meat, onions, tomatoes, green chillies, ginger, salt and ½ cup water in a pressure cooker and cook under pressure for 30 minutes.
- Stir in coconut-spice paste and boil till gravy thickens.
- Heat oil for tempering in a small pan and sprinkle in mustard seeds. When they start sputtering, add remaining ingredients and fry till shallots turn brown.
- Pour contents of pan into curry, mix well and serve with rice, pathiri or porotta.

Variation: Chicken can be used instead of mutton or beef. In this case do not pressure cook.

IRACHI VARATIATHU – I
Meat Cooked with Chopped Coconut

Serves: 6

A Christian dish.

1 kg mutton or beef
7 shallots, chopped
4 cloves garlic, chopped
3-cm piece ginger, chopped
1 stalk curry leaves
¼ fresh coconut, finely chopped
2 tsp white vinegar
1 tsp salt

91

Ground to a fine paste:

3 shallots, chopped
2 tsp red chilli powder
2 tsp coriander powder
½ tsp turmeric powder
½ tsp black pepper powder
A pinch of cumin seeds
A pinch of fennel seeds (badi saunf)
1 white cardamom, peeled
5-cm stick cinnamon, broken into pieces
3 cloves
4 tsp water

Tempering:

4 tbsp oil
1 tsp mustard seeds
1 medium-sized onion, chopped
1 stalk curry leaves

- Wash meat, drain and cut into 3-cm pieces.
- Place in a pressure cooker with ¾ cup water and all ingredients, except tempering. Cook under pressure for 30 minutes.
- Open cooker, simmer till gravy is nearly dry and remove from heat.
- Heat oil for tempering in a small pan and sprinkle in mustard seeds. When they start sputtering, add onion and curry leaves, and fry till onion turns translucent.
- Pour contents of pan into curry, mix well and serve with rice, pathiri or porotta.

IRACHI VARATIATHU – II
Meat Cooked with Milk

Serves: 4

A Christian dish.

500 gms boneless mutton or beef
1 cup ghee
3 medium-sized onions, chopped
6 shallots, chopped
2 stalks curry leaves
1 tsp powdered mustard seeds
1 tsp black pepper powder
1½ cups milk

Ground to a fine paste:
6 green chillies, chopped
1 tsp turmeric powder
1 tsp black pepper powder
1 tsp mustard seeds
3-cm piece ginger, chopped
1½ tbsp white vinegar
1 tsp salt
4 tsp water

- Wash meat, pat dry and cut into thin, 3-cm long strips.
- Rub spice paste into meat and marinate for an hour.
- Heat ghee in a kadhai and deep-fry meat in batches. Drain and set aside in a fresh pan.
- Add onions, shallots and curry leaves to kadhai, and fry till shallots turn brown. Add to meat.
- Mix spice powders with milk and stir into meat.
- Place pan with meat on high heat, bring to boil, lower heat and simmer till gravy thickens.
- Serve with rice, pathiri or porotta.

IRACHI VARATHATHU
Deep-fried Meat

Serves: 4

500 gms boneless mutton or beef
1 cup oil
8 green chillies, slit
½ medium-sized, fresh coconut, grated

Ground to a fine paste:
3 cloves garlic, chopped
3-cm piece ginger, chopped
3 tsp red chilli powder
1 tsp coriander powder
½ tsp turmeric powder
1 tsp black pepper powder
3-cm stick cinnamon, broken into pieces
2 cloves
1 tsp fennel seeds (badi saunf)
1 tsp salt
4 tsp water

- Wash meat, drain and cut into finger-sized strips.
- Place in a pressure cooker with scant ½ cup water and cook under pressure for 30 minutes.
- Drain off stock and use for some other purpose.
- Rub spice paste into meat and marinate for an hour.
- Heat oil in a kadhai and deep-fry meat in batches. Drain and set aside.
- Reduce oil to 2 tbsp, add green chillies and coconut, and fry, stirring constantly, till coconut turns brown.
- Mix in meat and serve.

THENGA ARACHA IRACHI KARI
Meat Curry with Coconut

Serves: 4

A Christian dish.

500 gms mutton or beef
2 tbsp oil
1 tsp mustard seeds
2 medium-sized onions, chopped
5 green chillies, slit
1 stalk curry leaves
1 tsp salt
4 medium-sized tomatoes, chopped
2-3 sprigs coriander leaves, chopped

Ground to a fine paste:
3-cm piece ginger, chopped
2 cloves garlic, chopped
3-cm stick cinnamon, broken into pieces
2 cloves
½ tsp fennel seeds (badi saunf)
3 tsp red chilli powder
1 tsp coriander powder
½ tsp turmeric powder
1 tsp black pepper powder
4 tsp water

Ground to a fine paste:
½ medium-sized, fresh coconut, grated
¾ cup water

- Wash meat, drain and cut into 3-cm pieces.
- Place in a pressure cooker with ¾ cup water and cook under pressure for 30 minutes.

95

- Heat oil in a pan and sprinkle in mustard seeds. When they start sputtering, add onions, green chillies and curry leaves, and fry till onions turn translucent.
- Mix in spice paste and fry, stirring constantly, for 5 minutes.
- Add salt and meat with its stock, and bring to boil.
- Stir in tomatoes, coriander leaves and coconut paste, simmer for 5 minutes and remove from heat.

THENGAPALUM THAIRUM CHERTHA ATTIRACHI KARI
Mutton Curry with Coconut Milk and Curd

Serves: 4

A Muslim dish.

500 gms mutton
4 tbsp oil
1 medium-sized onion, chopped
10 cloves
5-cm stick cinnamon, broken into pieces
6 white cardamoms, powdered
½ tsp turmeric powder
10 cloves garlic, chopped
5-cm piece ginger, chopped
1 tsp red chilli powder
1 tsp coriander powder
2 medium-sized tomatoes, chopped
2 cups coconut milk (1st extract; see p. 20)
1 tsp salt
¼ cup curd (not sour), whisked
4 green chillies, slit
1 tsp lime juice

1 sprig coriander leaves, chopped
1 stalk curry leaves

Ground to a fine paste:
¼ medium-sized, fresh coconut, grated
5 tbsp water

- Wash meat, drain and cut into 3-cm pieces.
- Heat oil in a pan, add onion and fry till translucent.
- Lower heat, add whole spices and cardamom powder, and fry for a minute till fragrant.
- Add turmeric, garlic, ginger, chilli powder and coriander powder (in this order), frying for a minute or so between each addition, and stirring constantly.
- Mix in tomatoes and ½ cup water, and cook till tomatoes are soft.
- Add meat and sauté well for 10 minutes.
- Mix coconut paste with coconut milk and add to meat.
- Cover pan and cook over low heat for 30 minutes, till meat is half done.
- Stir in salt, curd and green chillies, cover pan and continue to cook over low heat till meat is tender.
- Add lime juice, coriander leaves and curry leaves. Mix well and remove from heat.
- Serve with rice, pathiri, porotta, puttu, appam or idiappam.

ATTIRACHI PERALEN
Mutton Curry

Serves: 8

A Christian dish.

1 kg boneless mutton
2 tsp white vinegar
1 tsp salt
4 tbsp oil
1 tsp mustard seeds
1 medium-sized onion, chopped
10 cloves garlic, chopped
5-cm piece ginger, chopped
1 tsp plain flour (maida)

Ground to a fine paste:
1 tsp black pepper powder
2 white cardamoms, peeled
3 cloves
3-cm stick cinnamon, broken into pieces
½ tsp turmeric powder
1 tsp red chilli powder
2 tsp coriander powder
4 tsp water

- Wash meat, drain and cut into 4-cm long, 1-cm wide strips.
- Place in a pressure cooker with vinegar, salt and ¾ cup water, and cook under pressure for 30 minutes.
- Heat oil in a pan and sprinkle in mustard seeds. When they start sputtering, add onion and fry till translucent.
- Mix in garlic and ginger, and fry till the aroma of cooked garlic is released, stirring occasionally.

- Stir in spice paste and fry for 2 minutes.
- Add mutton with its stock and mix well.
- Combine flour with 3 tsp water and stir into pan. Cook over low heat, stirring occasionally, till gravy thickens.
- Serve with rice or porotta.

IRACHI MAPAS
Meat Curry with Coconut Milk

Serves: 4

A Christian dish.

500 gms mutton or beef
3 tsp red chilli powder
1 tsp black pepper powder
1 tsp coriander powder
1 tsp turmeric powder
3-cm stick cinnamon, powdered
2 cloves, powdered
A pinch of fennel powder (badi saunf)
1 tsp salt
1 stalk curry leaves
5-cm piece ginger, julienned
2 cloves garlic, chopped
4 green chillies, slit
2 medium-sized onions, sliced
2 cups coconut milk (1st extract; see p. 20)

Tempering:

1½ tbsp oil
1 tsp mustard seeds
2 shallots, chopped
1 stalk curry leaves

- Wash meat, drain and cut into 3-cm pieces.
- Place in a pressure cooker with scant ½ cup water, and cook under pressure for 30 minutes.
- Open cooker and add spice powders, salt, curry leaves, ginger, garlic, green chillies and onions.
- Bring to boil, lower heat and add coconut milk. Simmer over low heat for 2 minutes and remove from heat.
- Heat oil for tempering in a small pan and sprinkle in mustard seeds. When they start sputtering, add shallots and curry leaves, and fry till shallots turn brown.
- Pour contents of pan into curry, mix well and serve with rice, appam, puttu or idiappam.

Variation: The same recipe can be used to make hard boiled egg or chicken mapas, in which case there is no need for pressure-cooking. Duck's eggs are preferred to chicken eggs, since after being hard-boiled, they weather the cooking in the gravy well.

IRACHI CHERTHA KAPPA PUZHUKKU
Meat with Tapioca

Serves: 6

200 gms boneless mutton or beef
500 gms tapioca
½ tsp + 1 tsp salt
1 tbsp ghee
8 shallots, chopped
3 dry red chillies, torn into pieces
2 + 2 stalks curry leaves
½ tsp turmeric powder
1 tsp red chilli powder

- Wash meat, drain and cut into 3-cm pieces.
- Place in a pressure cooker with scant ½ cup water and cook under pressure for 30 minutes.
- Peel, clean and wash tapioca, and cut into 1-cm pieces.
- Place in a pan with water to cover completely. Bring to boil over high heat and cook till tender. (A knife or fork should pierce it easily.)
- Remove from heat, drain and mash with ½ tsp salt.
- Heat ghee in a pan, add shallots, red chillies and 2 stalks curry leaves, and fry till shallots turn brown.
- Add spice powders, 1 tsp salt, 2 stalks curry leaves, and meat with its stock. Mix well and cook over moderate heat for 2 minutes.
- Mix in tapioca and serve.

ATTIRACHI THORAN
Stir-fried Mince with Coconut

Serves: 4

A Christian dish.

500 gms mutton, minced
2 medium-sized onions, sliced
3 green chillies, slit
3-cm piece ginger, julienned
2 medium-sized tomatoes, chopped
1 tsp salt
1½ tbsp oil

Coarsely ground:

½ medium-sized, fresh coconut, grated
4 shallots, chopped
2 cloves garlic, chopped
6 dry red chillies, torn into pieces
1 tsp turmeric powder
1 tsp coriander powder
1 tsp black pepper powder
3-cm stick cinnamon, broken into pieces
2 cloves
½ tsp fennel seeds (badi saunf)

- Combine mince, onions, green chillies and ginger in a pressure cooker with scant ½ cup water and cook under pressure for 30 minutes.
- Open cooker, add tomatoes, salt and coconut-spice paste, and cook over high heat till dry, stirring constantly.
- Mix in oil and remove from heat.

ATTIRACHI KARI
Mutton Curry

Serves: 4

A Muslim dish.

500 gms mutton
3-cm piece ginger, chopped
1 tsp salt
2 tsp white vinegar
2 tbsp ghee
2 medium-sized onions, sliced
1 stalk curry leaves
2 sprigs coriander leaves, chopped

Ground to a fine paste:
½ medium-sized, fresh coconut, grated
4 shallots, chopped
3 cloves garlic, chopped
2 tsp coriander powder
4 tsp red chilli powder
1 tsp black pepper powder
1 tsp turmeric powder
5-cm stick cinnamon, broken into pieces
3 cloves
1 tsp fennel seeds (badi saunf)
¾ cup water

- Wash meat, drain and cut into 3-cm pieces.
- Place in a pressure cooker with ginger, salt, vinegar and scant ½ cup water, and cook under pressure for 30 minutes.
- Heat ghee in a pan, add onions and curry leaves, and fry till onions turn translucent.

- Mix in coconut-spice paste and bring to boil.
- Add coriander leaves and meat with its stock. Mix well and cook over low heat till gravy thickens.
- Serve with pathiri, porotta or rice.

MATTIRACHI PERALEN
Spicy Beef Curry

Serves: 8

A Christian dish.

1 kg boneless beef
4 tsp white vinegar
1 tsp salt
5-cm piece ginger, chopped
1¼ tsp turmeric powder
1½ tbsp + 1½ tbsp oil
2 medium-sized onions, chopped
4 cloves garlic, chopped
8 green chillies, slit
1 stalk curry leaves
1 tsp mustard seeds
1 tsp plain flour (maida)
1 tsp coriander powder
1 tsp black peppercorns, crushed

- Wash meat, drain and cut into 4-cm long, 1-cm wide strips.
- Place in a pressure cooker with vinegar, salt, ¾ cup water and half the ginger and turmeric, and cook under pressure for 30 minutes.
- Separate meat from stock and set aside.

- Heat 1½ tbsp oil in a pan, add onions, garlic, green chillies, curry leaves and remaining ginger, and fry till onions turn translucent. Remove from oil and set aside.
- Pour remaining oil into pan and sprinkle in mustard seeds. When they start sputtering, sprinkle in flour, coriander powder, pepper and remaining turmeric, and fry for 2 minutes, stirring constantly.
- Add meat and sauté for 5 minutes.
- Stir in reserved onion mixture and cook for 2 minutes more.
- Pour in stock, mix well and cook till gravy thickens.
- Serve with rice or porotta.

THENGA CHERTHA MATTIRACHI
MEZHUKKUPURATTI
Beef with Coconut

Serves: 4

A Christian dish.

500 gms beef
3 green chillies, slit
3-cm piece ginger, chopped
1 tsp black pepper powder
1 tsp salt
1½ tbsp oil
¼ medium-sized, fresh coconut, chopped
2 medium-sized onions, chopped
1 stalk curry leaves

Ground to a fine paste:
10 dry red chillies, torn into pieces
1 tsp coriander seeds
1 tsp turmeric powder
2 cloves
3-cm stick cinnamon, broken into pieces
¼ cup water

- Wash meat, drain and cut into 3-cm pieces.
- Place in a pressure cooker with green chillies, ginger, pepper, salt and ½ cup water, and cook under pressure for 30 minutes.
- Heat oil in a pan, add coconut and onions, and fry till coconut turns brown, stirring constantly.
- Mix in curry leaves and spice paste, and fry for 2 minutes, stirring constantly.
- Add meat with its stock and cook, stirring occasionally, till dry.

THALACHOR KARI
Brain Curry

Serves: 4

A Christian dish.

> 500 gms lambs' brains
> Juice of 3 limes
> 1 tsp salt
> 1½ tbsp oil
> 3 medium-sized onions, chopped
> 4 medium-sized tomatoes, chopped
> 2 tsp red chilli powder
> 1 tsp coriander powder
> ½ tsp turmeric powder
> 1 tsp black pepper powder
> 2 cups coconut milk (1st extract; see p. 20)

- Wash brains and keep whole.
- Dip in boiling hot water for 5 minutes. Drain and dip in cold water for 15 minutes. Drain again, remove membranes and wash well.
- Place whole brains in a pan with lime juice, salt and ¾ cup water, and cook over medium heat for 10 minutes.
- Drain and cut brains into small pieces.
- Heat oil in a pan, add onions and tomatoes, and fry till onions turn translucent.
- Sprinkle in spice powders and gently mix in brains with scant ½ cup water.
- Bring to boil and cook till almost dry.
- Stir in coconut milk and simmer over low heat for 2 minutes.
- Serve with porotta, pathiri, appam or idiappam.

ATTINKARAL KARI
Liver Curry

Serves: 4

A Christian dish.

500 gms lamb's liver
1½ tbsp oil
10 shallots, chopped
3-cm piece ginger, chopped
3 cloves
1 tsp salt

Ground to a fine paste:
3 cloves garlic, chopped
4 tsp red chilli powder
1 tsp black pepper powder
1 tsp turmeric powder
1 tsp cumin seeds
1½ tbsp white vinegar
4 tsp water

- Remove membrane from liver, wash well, drain and cut into 2-cm pieces.
- Heat oil in a pan, add shallots, ginger and cloves, and fry till shallots turn brown.
- Add liver, salt and spice paste and mix well.
- Stir in scant ½ cup water and cook over low heat till liver is tender and gravy thickens.
- Serve with rice or porotta.

The Essential Kerala Cookbook

PANNIYIRACHI VINDALOO
Pork Vindaloo

Serves: 4

This dish, and the next, come from the Latin Christian community. The Malayalis who converted to Christianity after the arrival of the Portuguese are called Latin Christians. Hence, the similarity to the more well-known Goan dishes.

In the Malayali version, there are certain notable additions to the ingredients—shallots, cardamoms, poppy seeds and a liberal measure of dry red chillies.

500 gms pork
2 tsp salt
4 tbsp oil

Marinade:

1¾ cups white vinegar
5 shallots, chopped
2 cloves garlic, chopped
5-cm piece ginger, finely chopped
3-cm stick cinnamon, powdered
2 cloves, powdered
8 white cardamoms, peeled and powdered
10 black peppercorns, powdered

Ground to a fine paste:

5 shallots, chopped
12 dry red chillies
2 tsp coriander powder
2 tsp poppy seeds (khus-khus)
2 tsp cumin seeds
¼ cup water

109

- Wash pork, pat dry and cut into 3-cm pieces.
- Rub salt over pork and set aside for an hour.
- Combine ingredients for marinade and pour over pork, ensuring that it completely covers the pork. Keep covered for 3 days, turning it twice a day, without refrigerating. (If the pork is completely covered with marinade, it should not go bad even in summer. However, if the weather is very hot, you can refrigerate it and bring to room temperature before cooking.)
- Heat oil in a pan, add spice paste and fry for 2 minutes, stirring constantly.
- Drain pork, add to pan and sauté for 5 minutes.
- Stir in ¾ cup hot water, cover pan and cook over low heat, stirring occasionally, for 30-40 minutes, till tender.
- Serve with rice or porotta.

PANNIYIRACHI KOOTAN
Pork Curry

Serves: 8

1 kg pork
2 tbsp oil
4 medium-sized onions, chopped
2 medium-sized tomatoes, chopped
1 tbsp white vinegar
2 tsp salt

Ground to a fine paste:
2½ tbsp sultanas (kishmish)
1 whole head garlic, chopped
5-cm piece ginger, chopped
4 green chillies, chopped
A walnut-sized ball of seedless tamarind
1 tsp black pepper powder
2 tsp turmeric powder
6 cloves
5-cm stick cinnamon, broken into pieces
1 tsp mustard seeds
2 tbsp water

- Wash pork, drain and cut into 3-cm pieces.
- Place in a pressure cooker with ¾ cup water and cook under pressure for 30 minutes.
- Strain and reserve pork and stock.
- Heat oil in a pan, add onions and tomatoes, and fry till onions turn translucent.
- Mix in spice paste and fry for 2 minutes.
- Add pork and fry till brown, stirring occasionally.
- Stir in stock, vinegar, salt and ¾ cup water. Cover pan and cook over low heat for 30-40 minutes, till pork is tender and gravy thickens.
- Serve with rice or porotta.

THENGAYUM KASUANDIPARIPPUM CHERTHA KOZHI KARI
Chicken Curry with Coconut and Cashewnut

Serves: 8

A Muslim dish.

1 kg chicken
2 tbsp oil
2 shallots, chopped
5 medium-sized onions, chopped
4 cloves garlic, chopped
5-cm piece ginger, chopped
5 green chillies, chopped
1 stalk curry leaves, chopped
4 tsp coriander powder
1½ tsp red chilli powder
1 tsp turmeric powder
1½ tsp Malayali five-spice powder (see p. 32)
3 medium-sized tomatoes, chopped
1 tsp salt
1 stalk coriander leaves, chopped

Coconut-shallot paste:
2 tbsp oil
½ medium-sized, fresh coconut, grated
8 shallots, chopped

Ground to a fine paste:
2½ tbsp unsalted, split cashewnuts
4 tsp water

- Heat oil for coconut-shallot paste in a frying pan, add coconut and shallots, and fry till brown. Cool and grind with ¾ cup water.

- Cut chicken into 3-cm pieces and wash.
- Heat oil in a pan, add shallots and onions, and fry till translucent.
- Add garlic, ginger, green chillies and curry leaves, and fry till the aroma of cooked garlic is released.
- Sprinkle in spice powders and fry for 2 minutes, stirring constantly.
- Mix in tomatoes and cook for 5 minutes longer.
- Add salt and chicken, mix well, pour in ¾ cup water and cook over low heat for about 15 minutes, till chicken is tender.
- Add coconut-shallot paste, bring to boil and add cashewnut paste and coriander leaves. Mix well and serve with ghee rice.

Note: To serve with pathiri substitute ½ cup coconut milk for the coconut-shallot paste and add water only if necessary.

THENGAPAL CHERTHA VARUTHA KOZHI KARI
Chicken Curry with Coconut Milk

Serves: 4

A Muslim dish.

500 gms chicken
1½ tbsp + 5½ tbsp ghee
2 medium-sized onions, sliced
2 medium-sized potatoes, sliced
2 cups coconut milk (1st extract; see p. 20)
1 tsp salt
6 green chillies, slit
2 stalks curry leaves
2 sprigs coriander leaves, chopped

Ground to a fine paste:
8 shallots, chopped
6 cloves garlic, chopped
8 dry red chillies, torn into pieces
3 cloves
2 x 8-cm sticks cinnamon, broken into pieces
20 black peppercorns
2 tsp poppy seeds (khus-khus)
1 tsp coriander powder
1 tsp turmeric powder
¼ cup water

- Cut chicken into 5-cm pieces, wash well and pat dry.
- Rub ground paste into chicken and marinate for 20-30 minutes.
- Heat 1½ tbsp ghee in a kadhai, add onions and potatoes, and fry till potatoes are cooked and onions

turn translucent. Remove from kadhai, drain and set aside. Reserve ghee in the kadhai.
- Place chicken in a fresh pan with coconut milk and salt. Place pan over low heat and cook for about 10 minutes, till chicken is half done.
- Add green chillies, curry leaves and coriander leaves, and continue cooking till gravy thickens. Remove from heat and separate chicken pieces from gravy.
- Add 5½ tbsp ghee to reserved ghee in the kadhai and place over high heat. Add chicken pieces and fry till brown. Mix in reserved potatoes, onions and gravy.
- Serve with rice, porotta, appam or idiappam.

KOZHI PERALEN
Spicy Chicken Curry

Serves: 8

A Christian dish.

1 kg chicken
½ cup oil
10 shallots, chopped
½ tsp turmeric powder
2 medium-sized tomatoes, chopped
3 green chillies, slit
1 tsp mustard seeds
½ tsp sugar
2 tsp white vinegar
½ tsp salt

Marinade:

2 tsp white vinegar
½ tsp salt

Ground to a fine paste:

5-cm piece ginger, chopped
6 cloves garlic, chopped
3 tsp red chilli powder
1 tsp coriander powder
A pinch of fenugreek seeds (methi)
4 tsp water

- Cut chicken into 3-cm pieces, wash well and pat dry.
- Combine ingredients for marinade, rub into chicken and marinate for an hour.
- Heat oil in a pan, add shallots and fry till brown.
- Sprinkle in turmeric and fry for a minute, stirring constantly.
- Lower heat, remove shallots from pan and reserve.
- Add tomatoes to pan, fry for 5 minutes, remove from pan and add to shallots.
- Add green chillies to pan, fry for 2 minutes, remove from pan and add to shallots and tomatoes.
- Sprinkle mustard seeds into pan. When they start sputtering, add chicken with its marinade and ¾ cup water. Cover pan and cook for about 10 minutes till chicken is half done and gravy begins to thicken.
- Mix sugar with vinegar and stir in with salt and spice paste. Simmer for 2 minutes till gravy thickens.
- Add reserved shallots, tomatoes, and green chillies. Mix well and continue to simmer for 5-10 minutes longer, till chicken is tender and coated with gravy.
- Serve with rice, porotta or pathiri.

KASUANDIPARIPPUM THAIRUM
CHERTHA KOZHI KARI
Chicken Curry with Curd and Cashewnut

Serves: 8

A Muslim dish.

1 kg chicken
1 tbsp + 1½ tbsp oil
2½ tbsp unsalted cashewnuts
4 medium-sized onions, finely chopped
5-cm stick cinnamon
4 tsp red chilli powder

Marinade:
½ cup curd, whisked
1 tsp turmeric powder
1 tsp salt

Ground to a creamy paste:
2½ tbsp unsalted cashewnuts
3 tbsp curd

- Cut chicken into 5-cm pieces, wash well and pat dry.
- Combine ingredients for marinade, rub into chicken and marinate for an hour.
- Heat 1 tbsp oil in a pan, add cashewnuts and fry till brown. Drain and set aside.
- Pour remaining oil into pan and heat. Add onions and cinnamon, and fry till onions turn translucent.
- Mix chilli powder with ¾ cup water and stir in.
- Bring to boil and add chicken with its marinade. Mix well, cover pan and cook over low heat for 15-20 minutes,

till chicken is tender and gravy thickens.
- Stir in cashewnut paste and cook for 5 minutes longer.
- Garnish with reserved cashewnuts and serve with porotta, pathiri or rice.

KOZHI VARATHATHU
Chicken-fry

Serves: 8

1 kg boneless chicken breast
1 cup oil

Marinade:

1½ tsp turmeric powder
4 tsp red chilli powder
2 tsp coriander powder
Juice of 1 lime
1 tsp salt

- Cut chicken into 5-cm pieces, wash well and pat dry.
- Combine ingredients for marinade, rub into chicken and marinate for 30 minutes.
- Heat oil in a kadhai over moderate heat, and deep fry chicken in batches till tender and brown.

NIRACHA KOZHI
Stuffed Chicken

Serves: 8

A Muslim dish, it is said to have a connection to the Arab khouzi. The latter, however, is spit roasted or cooked in water in a sealed pan, and rice and nuts are the main ingredients for the stuffing. In this dish the whole chicken is deep fried, and neither rice nor nuts are used.

1 kg chicken with skin, kept whole
3½ cups oil

Stuffing:

4 eggs, hard-boiled
1 tsp red chilli powder
½ tsp salt
3 tbsp oil
3 medium-sized onions, chopped
6 green chillies, chopped
3-cm piece ginger, chopped
4 cloves garlic, chopped

Ground to a fine paste:

3-cm piece ginger, chopped
6 green chillies, chopped
4 cloves garlic, chopped
1 stalk curry leaves
1 tsp red chilli powder
½ tsp black pepper powder
1 tsp turmeric powder
¼ tsp Malayali five-spice powder (see p. 32)
½ tsp salt
4 tsp water

- Wash chicken thoroughly inside and out, and set aside to drain.
- To prepare stuffing, peel eggs and score with a knife. Combine chilli powder and salt, and roll eggs in mixture to coat thoroughly.
- Heat oil in a pan and fry eggs lightly. Remove from oil, drain and set aside.
- Add onions to pan and fry till translucent.
- Mix in green chillies, ginger and garlic, and fry for 5 minutes, stirring constantly.
- Stuff chicken with eggs and onion mixture. Close by sewing it with needle and thread.
- Rub spice paste over chicken and marinate for 2 hours.
- Heat oil in a kadhai over moderate heat and deep fry chicken, turning it around frequently, so that it is evenly cooked and brown.
- Serve with rice, porotta or pathiri.

KOZHIPPIDI
Anna Pathiri

Serves: 4

A Muslim dish.

Presumably, the second name for this dish comes from the size of the pathiri, which is more or less equal to the old anna coin.

Pathiri:

2½ cups parboiled rice
½ medium-sized, fresh coconut, grated
4 shallots, chopped
A pinch of cumin seeds
½ tsp salt
¾ cup water

Coconut-shallot paste:

2 tbsp oil
1 medium-sized, fresh coconut, grated
4 shallots, chopped
1½ cups water

Curry:

500 gms chicken
1 medium-sized onion, chopped
2 green chillies, chopped
3-cm piece ginger, chopped
6 cloves garlic, chopped
1 stalk curry leaves, chopped
1 tsp red chilli powder
1 tsp turmeric powder
1 tsp coriander powder
1 tsp Malayali five-spice powder (see p. 32)
½ tsp salt

Pathiri:
- Soak rice in hot water for 8 hours. Drain and grind with remaining ingredients for pathiri to a thick dough.
- Pinch off marble-sized balls of dough and shape between your palms into 3-cm round pathiri.
- Spread pathiri on a steel plate in overlapping layers and steam for 10-15 minutes. Allow to cool, sprinkle cold water over them and separate them.

Coconut-shallot paste:
- Heat oil in a pan, add coconut and fry, stirring constantly, till brown. Remove coconut from oil and grind with remaining ingredients to a fine paste.
- Reserve pan with oil.

Curry:
- Cut chicken into 7-cm pieces, wash well and drain.
- Heat pan containing reserved oil, add onion and fry till translucent.
- Lower heat, add green chillies, ginger, garlic and curry leaves, and fry till the aroma of cooked garlic is released.
- Sprinkle in spice powders and salt, mix well and fry for 2 minutes. Stir in chicken and 1½ cups water. Cover pan and cook over low heat for 20 minutes till chicken is tender.
- Mix in coconut-shallot paste and bring to boil.
- Add steamed pathiri and remove from heat.
- Serve immediately with drumstick leaf curry.

Variation: The dish can also be cooked with mutton or beef.

KOZHI KOOTAN
Chicken Curry without Coconut

Serves: 4

500 gms chicken
4 tbsp oil
3 medium-sized onions, chopped
3-cm piece ginger, julienned
1 tsp salt
4 medium-sized tomatoes, chopped
1 stalk curry leaves

Ground to a fine paste:
10 shallots, chopped
3-cm piece ginger, chopped
8 cloves garlic, chopped
10 dry red chillies, torn into pieces
1 tsp cumin seeds
1 tsp fennel seeds (badi saunf)
20 black peppercorns
½ tsp turmeric powder
¼ cup water

- Cut chicken into 5-cm pieces, wash well and drain.
- Heat oil in a pan, add onions and fry till translucent.
- Mix in ground paste and fry for 2 minutes. Remove half the onion-spice paste from pan and set aside.
- Add chicken, ginger and salt to pan and sauté till chicken is cooked.
- Mix in tomatoes, curry leaves and ¾ cup water, and cook over low heat till oil separates.
- Stir in reserved onion-spice paste and remove from heat.
- Serve with rice, porotta, appam or idiappam.

123

THENGAPAL CHERTHA THARAVU KOOTAN
Duck Curry with Coconut Milk

Serves: 8

A Christian dish.

1 kg duck
2 tbsp oil
2 medium-sized onions, sliced
5-cm piece ginger, chopped
12 cloves garlic, chopped
6 green chillies, slit
4 tsp white vinegar
1 tsp salt
2 cups coconut milk (1st extract; see p. 20)

Ground to a fine paste:
5-cm stick cinnamon, broken into pieces
6 cloves
4 white cardamoms, peeled
2 tsp coriander powder
2 tsp red chilli powder
½ tsp turmeric powder
½ tsp black pepper powder
2 tbsp water

Tempering:
1 tsp ghee
1 tsp mustard seeds
4 shallots, chopped
1 stalk curry leaves

• Cut duck into 5-cm pieces, wash well and drain.

- Heat oil in a pan, add onions, ginger, garlic and green chillies, and fry till onions turn translucent.
- Mix in duck, vinegar, salt, spice paste and ¾ cup water. Cover pan and cook over low heat till duck is half done.
- Pour in coconut milk and bring to boil. Lower heat and simmer gently till duck is cooked and gravy has thickened.
- Heat ghee for tempering in a small pan and sprinkle in mustard seeds. When they start sputtering, add remaining ingredients and fry till shallots turn brown.
- Pour contents of pan into curry, mix well and serve with rice or porotta.

VARUTHARACHA THARAVU KARI
Spicy Duck Curry

Serves: 8

A Christian dish.

1 kg duck
½ cup oil
3 medium-sized onions, finely sliced
2 medium-sized potatoes, finely sliced
4 shallots, chopped
1 tsp plain flour (maida)
1 tsp salt

Spice paste:

½ tbsp oil
20 dry red chillies, seeded
6 shallots, chopped

125

6 cloves garlic, chopped
3-cm piece ginger, chopped
1 tsp poppy seeds (khus-khus)
½ tsp cumin seeds
½ tsp fennel seeds (badi saunf)
2 white cardamoms, peeled
3-cm stick cinnamon, broken into pieces
2 cloves
2 tsp white vinegar
¼ cup water

- Heat ½ tbsp oil for spice paste in a pan and fry red chillies till fragrant. Cool and grind to a smooth paste with remaining ingredients for spice paste.
- Cut duck into 5-cm pieces, wash well and pat dry.
- Mix spice paste into duck and marinate for 2 hours.
- Place duck in a pressure cooker with scant 1 cup water and cook under pressure for 15 minutes.
- Strain and reserve stock.
- Heat oil in a pan, add duck and sauté till brown. Remove from pan and set aside.
- Add onions and potatoes to pan and fry till onions turn translucent. Remove onions and potatoes from pan and set aside.
- Reduce oil to 2 tbsp, add shallots and fry till brown.
- Sprinkle in flour, mix well and add duck and reserved onions, potatoes and stock. Mix well, bring to boil and simmer till potatoes are tender and gravy thickens.
- Serve with rice or porotta.

THARAVUMUTTA THORAN
Scrambled Ducks' Eggs with Coconut

Serves: 6

This is a popular form of preparing eggs in Kerala. It is generally served with rice when fish and meat are not available. It can also be made with chicken eggs.

1½ tbsp oil
1 tsp mustard seeds
2 shallots, chopped
1 stalk curry leaves
1 tsp salt
6 ducks' eggs, well beaten

Ground to a coarse paste:
½ medium-sized, fresh coconut, grated
4 shallots, chopped
5 green chillies, chopped
A pinch of cumin seeds
½ tsp turmeric powder

- Heat oil in a pan and sprinkle in mustard seeds. When they start sputtering, add shallots and curry leaves, and fry till shallots turn brown.
- Lower heat, add coconut paste and salt, and fry for 2 minutes.
- Pour in eggs and stir continuously over low heat till scrambled and dry.
- Serve immediately with rice.

Variation: This dish can also be prepared with chicken eggs, or as an omelette on a tava or griddle.

127

Fish and shellfish

The general perception is that because of its long coastline seafood has always been widely popular throughout Kerala. However this is a development which is probably about six decades old. Until then, the lack of mechanical means of transport, good roads and the difficult terrain, inevitably confined the consumption of seafood to the coastal areas.

People living away from the coast relied mostly on freshwater or dried seafood. This divide still remains in a cultural sense. While the people of the coast believe that freshwater fish consume dirt and therefore taste of mud, the people living inland find seafood abhorrent because of its smell. Fortunately, these prejudices are fast disappearing.

Every kind of seafood and freshwater fish is eaten by the Malayali. Because of easy availability, seer, mackerel, sardine, rohu, mullet and sole are widely consumed.

As a rule, fish that have only a central bone are used in curries. The more bony ones are fried. This distinction should be kept in mind when trying out the recipes.

A species that is unique to Kerala and highly popular is the pearl spot (karimeen in Malayalam) that lives in the brackish backwaters. Recipes that call for the use of karimeen are identified in the text. A passable substitute for karimeen is pomfret.

Sun-dried seafood is also used. It is heavily coated with salt before drying. To re-hydrate it and to remove excess salt it is washed and soaked in water before cooking. Fish should be soaked for an hour, while thirty minutes should do the trick for prawns.

Though many of the fish dishes are common to all communities in Kerala, some are specific to the Christian and Muslim culinary traditions.

THENGA ARACHA MEEN KARI
Fish Curry with Coconut

Serves: 6

500 gms fish
1 medium-sized onion, chopped
3-cm piece ginger, chopped
2 green chillies, slit
3 petals cambodge, torn into pieces
4 tsp red chilli powder
1 tsp coriander powder
½ tsp turmeric powder
1 tsp black pepper powder
1½ tsp salt

Ground to a fine paste:

½ coconut, grated
2 shallots, chopped
2 cloves garlic, chopped
½ tsp cumin seeds
½ tsp turmeric powder
¾ cup water

Tempering:

1½ tbsp oil
1 tsp mustard seeds
1 tsp fenugreek seeds (methi)
2 shallots, chopped
2 stalks curry leaves

- Clean fish, cut into 3-cm pieces and wash.
- Place fish, onion, ginger, green chillies, cambodge, spice powders, salt, and ¾ cup water in a pan and cook over low heat for 10 minutes.
- Stir in coconut paste, bring to boil and remove from heat.

- Heat oil for tempering in a small pan and sprinkle in mustard seeds. When they start sputtering, add remaining ingredients and fry till shallots turn brown.
- Pour contents of pan into curry, mix gently and serve.

NADAN MEEN KARI
Country-style Fish Curry

Serves: 6

500 gms fish
1½ tbsp + ½ tbsp oil
1 tsp mustard seeds
1 tsp fenugreek seeds (methi)
5 dry red chillies, torn into pieces
5 green chillies, slit
3-cm piece ginger, chopped
6 cloves garlic, chopped
10 shallots, chopped
2 stalks curry leaves
1 tsp turmeric powder
1 tsp salt
3 petals cambodge, torn into pieces and soaked in scant 1 cup water

- Clean fish, cut into 3-cm pieces and wash.
- Heat 1½ tbsp oil in a pan and sprinkle in mustard seeds. When they start sputtering, add fenugreek, red chillies, green chillies, ginger, garlic, shallots and curry leaves, and fry till shallots turn brown.
- Stir in turmeric, salt and cambodge with its soaking liquid. Add fish, cover pan and cook over low heat till fish is tender and gravy thickens.
- Gently mix in ½ tbsp oil and serve.

MEEN VEVICHATHU
Spicy Fish Curry

Serves: 6

500 gms fish
1½ tbsp oil
1 tsp mustard seeds
1 tsp fenugreek seeds (methi)
2 shallots, chopped
3 green chillies, slit
5-cm piece ginger, chopped
2 stalks curry leaves
2 tsp salt
3 petals cambodge, torn into pieces and soaked in 5 tbsp water

Ground to a paste:
5 shallots, chopped
2 cloves garlic, chopped
5-cm stick cinnamon, broken into pieces
2 cloves
½ tsp fennel seeds (badi saunf)
4 tsp red chilli powder
2 tsp coriander powder
1 tsp turmeric powder
1 tsp black pepper powder
4 tsp water

- Clean fish, cut into 5-cm pieces and wash.
- Heat oil in a pan and sprinkle in mustard seeds. When they start sputtering add fenugreek and shallots, and fry till shallots turn brown.
- Add green chillies, ginger, curry leaves and salt, and fry for 5 minutes, stirring constantly.
- Mix in spice paste and fry for 2 minutes.
- Add fish and cambodge with its soaking liquid and cook over low heat for 10 minutes.

MEEN KUZHAMBU
Mashed Fish Curry with Coconut Milk

Serves: 6

A Christian dish.

500 gms fish fillet
6 shallots, chopped
6 green chillies, chopped
3 cloves garlic, chopped
3-cm piece ginger, chopped
½ tsp turmeric powder
1 tsp salt
1½ tbsp oil
1 tsp mustard seeds
1½ tsp white vinegar
¾ cup coconut milk (1st extract; see p. 20)

Ground to a fine paste:
½ medium-sized, fresh coconut, grated
¾ cup water

- Clean fish, cut into 1-cm pieces and wash.
- Place in a pan with ¾ cup water and cook over low heat till tender.
- Mash fish lightly. Mix in shallots, green chillies, garlic, ginger, turmeric and salt, and simmer for 10 minutes.
- Heat oil in a small pan and sprinkle in mustard seeds. When they start sputtering, add coconut paste and fry for 5 minutes, stirring constantly.
- Gently mix into fish and cook over low heat till it boils.
- Pour in vinegar and coconut milk, mix gently and remove from heat.
- Serve with rice, porotta or kappa puzhukku.

VARUTHA MEEN PALUKARI
Fried Fish Curry with Coconut Milk

Serves: 6

A Christian dish.

500 gms fish
1 cup oil
1 tsp mustard seeds
2 medium-sized onions, chopped
4 green chillies, chopped
2 stalks curry leaves
A walnut-sized ball of seedless tamarind soaked in 5 tbsp water
1 tsp salt
1 cup coconut milk (1st extract; see p. 20)

Ground to a fine paste:
4 shallots, chopped
3-cm piece ginger, chopped
4 cloves garlic, chopped
4 tsp red chilli powder
1 tsp coriander powder
1 tsp turmeric powder
1 tsp salt
4 tsp water

- Clean fish, cut into 3-cm pieces, wash and drain well.
- Rub half the spice paste into fish and marinate for an hour.
- Heat oil in a kadhai and deep-fry fish. Remove fish from kadhai, drain and set aside.
- Reduce oil to 2 tbsp and sprinkle in mustard seeds. When they start sputtering, add onions, green chillies and curry leaves, and fry till onions turn translucent.

- Extract tamarind pulp and strain into pan. Stir in salt and remaining spice paste, and fry for 5 minutes, stirring constantly.
- Add fish and coconut milk. Mix gently, remove from heat and serve with rice or porotta.

MEEN MAPAS
Fish Curry with Coconut Milk

Serves: 6

A Christian dish.

500 gms fish
1½ tbsp oil
1 tsp mustard seeds
½ tsp fenugreek seeds (methi)
1 medium-sized onion, chopped
4 green chillies, slit
12 cloves garlic, chopped
3-cm piece ginger, chopped
1 stalk curry leaves
3 petals cambodge, torn into pieces and soaked in ¾ cup water
1 tsp salt
¾ cup coconut milk (1st extract; see p. 20)

Mixed together:
½ tsp black pepper powder
½ tsp turmeric powder
½ tsp red chilli powder
2 tsp coriander powder
4 tbsp water

- Clean fish, cut into 3-cm pieces and wash.
- Heat oil in a pan and sprinkle in mustard seeds. When

they start sputtering, add fenugreek, onion, green chillies, garlic, ginger, and curry leaves, and fry till onion turns translucent.

- Mix in spice paste and fry over low heat for 5 minutes, stirring constantly.
- Add cambodge with its soaking liquid and bring to boil.
- Add fish and salt, mix gently and cook over low heat till fish is tender and gravy thickens.
- Pour in coconut milk, bring to boil and remove from heat.
- Serve with rice, puttu or pathiri.

MEEN THEEYAL
Fish Curry with Shallots and Fried Coconut

Serves: 6

Theeyal is actually a style used for cooking certain vegetables. But as this recipe shows, the style can also be used in preparing fish.

500 gms fish
5 shallots, chopped
2 green chillies, slit
3-cm piece ginger, chopped
2 tsp red chilli powder
½ tsp turmeric powder
1 tsp salt
3 petals cambodge, torn into pieces

Coconut-spice paste:

1 tbsp oil
1 medium-sized, fresh coconut, grated
5 shallots, chopped
10 dry red chillies, torn into pieces
1 stalk curry leaves
1 tsp coriander seeds
1 tsp black pepper powder
2 cloves garlic, chopped
½ tsp turmeric powder

Tempering:

1 tbsp oil
1 tsp mustard seeds
1 tsp fenugreek seeds (methi)
2 shallots, chopped
1 stalk curry leaves

- Heat 1 tbsp oil for coconut-spice paste in a frying pan and fry coconut with remaining ingredients except garlic and turmeric, till coconut turns brown. Allow to cool, mix in garlic and turmeric, and grind to a fine paste with 1½ cups water.
- Clean fish, cut into 5-cm pieces and wash.
- Place in a pan with shallots, green chillies, ginger, spice powders, salt, cambodge and ¾ cup water, and cook over low heat for 10 minutes.
- Mix in coconut-spice paste and bring to boil over high heat. Lower heat, simmer till gravy thickens and remove from heat.
- Heat oil for tempering in a small pan and sprinkle in mustard seeds. When they start sputtering, add remaining ingredients and fry till shallots turn brown.
- Pour contents of pan into curry, mix gently and serve.

MEEN POLLICHATHU – I
Fish in Banana Leaves

Serves: 4

A Christian dish.

2 large banana leaves
500 gms whole fish (pearl spot/pomfret)
1 cup oil
2 medium-sized onions, chopped
4 green chillies, chopped
5-cm piece ginger, chopped
8 cloves garlic, chopped
A walnut-sized ball of seedless tamarind soaked in 5 tbsp water
½ tsp turmeric powder

3 tsp red chilli powder

Marinade:

Juice of 2 limes
½ tsp turmeric powder
1 tsp salt

- Clean banana leaves with a damp cloth on both sides, dry and pass over a live flame to make them pliable. Cut into pieces large enough to wrap a whole fish.
- Clean fish, keep whole, wash and drain thoroughly.
- Combine ingredients for marinade, rub into fish and marinate for 20 minutes.
- Heat oil in a frying pan and deep fry fish for about 5 minutes on each side. Remove fish from pan, drain and set aside.
- Reduce oil to 2 tbsp and add onions, green chillies, ginger and garlic, and fry till onions turn translucent.
- Extract tamarind pulp and strain in. Sprinkle in spice powders and boil till mixture thickens.
- Coat fish with mixture and stuff with remaining mixture. Wrap fish in banana leaves, using toothpicks to secure the parcels.
- Roast on a hot tava or griddle on each side for 2-5 minutes or place in a steamer for 2-5 minutes, till banana leaves turns blackish-brown.

141

MEEN POLLICHATHU – II
Fish in Banana Leaves

Serves: 8

A Christian dish.

4 large banana leaves
1 kg whole fish (pearl spot/pomfret)
½ cup oil
15 shallots, chopped
4 green chillies, chopped
12 cloves garlic, chopped
1 stalk curry leaves
1 tsp mustard seeds
½ cup coconut milk (1st extract; see p. 20)
3 petals cambodge, torn into pieces and soaked in 3 tbsp water

Marinade:

1 tsp black pepper powder
½ tsp turmeric powder
1 tsp salt

Mixed together:

1 tsp black pepper powder
½ tsp turmeric powder
2 tsp coriander powder
2 tsp red chilli powder
4 tsp water

- Clean banana leaves with a damp cloth on both sides, dry and pass over a live flame to make them pliable. Cut into pieces large enough to wrap a whole fish.
- Clean fish, keep whole, wash, drain thoroughly, and score with a knife on both sides.

- Combine ingredients for marinade, rub into fish and marinate for 30 minutes.
- Heat oil in a frying pan, add shallots, green chillies, garlic and curry leaves, and fry till shallots turn brown. Remove from oil and set aside.
- Place fish in pan and fry on each side for about 5 minutes till brown. Remove from pan, drain and set aside.
- Reduce oil to 2 tbsp and add mustard seeds. When they start sputtering, add spice paste and fry for about 2 minutes.
- Add fish, coconut milk and cambodge with its soaking liquid. Mix gently, cover pan and bring to boil.
- Open pan, gently stir in reserved shallot mixture and cook over low heat till gravy is almost dry.
- Remove from heat and wrap fish in banana leaves.
- Roast on a hot tava or griddle on each side for 2-5 minutes or place in a steamer for 2-5 minutes, till banana leaves turns blackish-brown.

MEEN / CHEMMEEN MOILY – I
Seafood Moily

Serves: 6

A Christian dish.

500 gms seafood (pearl spot/pomfret/prawns)
1 cup oil
2 medium-sized onions, chopped
4 green chillies, chopped
3-cm piece ginger, chopped
2 medium-sized tomatoes, chopped
1 stalk curry leaves
1 cup coconut milk (1st extract; see p. 20)

Marinade:

Juice of 2 limes
1 tsp turmeric powder
1 tsp salt

Ground to a fine paste:

2 cloves garlic, chopped
3 cloves
3-cm stick cinnamon, broken into pieces
1 tsp fennel (badi saunf)
3 tsp red chilli powder
2 tsp coriander powder
2 tsp black pepper powder
4 tsp water

- Clean fish (if used), cut into 5-cm pieces, wash and drain. Shell prawns (if used), remove heads, devein, wash and drain.
- Combine ingredients for marinade, mix in seafood and

marinate for 20 minutes.
- Drain seafood and reserve any marinade left over.
- Heat oil in a kadhai, add seafood and fry. (5-10 minutes for fish; 5 minutes for prawns.) Remove from oil, drain and set aside.
- Reduce oil to 2 tbsp, add onions, green chillies, ginger, tomato and curry leaves, and fry till onions turn brown.
- Stir in ground paste and fry for 2 minutes.
- Add seafood with reserved marinade and scant ½ cup water. Mix gently, cover pan and cook over low heat for 5 minutes.
- Stir in coconut milk and remove from heat.
- Serve with appam, pathiri or idiappam.

MEEN / CHEMMEEN MOILY – II
Seafood Moily

Serves: 6

A Christian dish.

500 gms seafood (pearl spot/pomfret/prawns)
2 medium-sized onions, chopped
2 medium-sized tomatoes, chopped
12 cloves garlic, chopped
1-cm piece ginger, julienned
4 green chillies, slit and seeded
2 stalks curry leaves
1 tsp turmeric powder
1 tsp salt
2 tbsp lime juice
1¼ cups coconut milk (1st extract; see p. 20)

Tempering:

2 tbsp oil
1 tsp mustard seeds

- Clean fish (if used), cut into 5-cm pieces, wash and drain. Shell prawns (if used), remove heads, devein, wash and drain.
- Arrange onions, tomatoes, garlic, ginger, green chillies and curry leaves, in the order given, in layers in a pan. Arrange seafood on top. Sprinkle with turmeric, salt and lime juice, and pour in ¾ cup water.
- Cover pan, place over moderate heat and bring to boil. Lower heat and simmer for 10 minutes.
- Add coconut milk, simmer for 2 minutes longer and remove from heat.
- Heat oil for tempering in a small pan and sprinkle in mustard seeds. When they start sputtering, pour contents of pan into moily and mix gently.
- Serve with appam, idiappam or pathiri.

MEEN POLLICHATHUM MOILY CHARUM
Moily with Fish Steamed in Banana Leaves

Serves: 4

This dish combines two well-known methods of Malayali culinary practice, though it has no claims to tradition.

4 whole fish, about 20 cm in size (pearl spot/pomfret)
2 large banana leaves
Moily curry prepared as given in meen / chemmeen moily – II (see p. 145) substituting 2 tsp powdered sun-dried prawns for the seafood

Ground to a fine paste:
6 sprigs coriander leaves
4 green chillies, chopped
2 cloves garlic, chopped
3-cm piece ginger, chopped
A walnut-sized ball of seedless tamarind
1 tsp cumin powder
A pinch of asafoetida powder (hing)
1 tsp salt
4 tsp water

- Clean fish, keep whole, wash and drain thoroughly.
- Coat fish with ground paste and stuff with any remaining paste.
- Clean banana leaves with a damp cloth on both sides, dry and pass over a live flame to make them pliable. Cut into pieces large enough to wrap fish.
- Wrap fish in banana leaves, using toothpicks to secure the parcels, and steam for 2-5 minutes, till banana leaves turn blackish-brown.

- To serve, open parcels, place fish in a dish and pour moily curry over them.

Note: The steamed fish can be served as a dish by itself.

MANGA CHERTHA MATHI KARI
Sardine Curry with Unripe Mango

Serves: 6

This curry does not use either tamarind or cambodge. The sour taste is provided by the mango.

25 sardines
1 large unripe, sour mango, peeled and sliced
1 medium-sized onion, sliced
12 green chillies, slit
3-cm piece ginger, sliced
15 curry leaves
1 tsp salt
¾ tsp oil

Ground to a fine paste:
8 cloves garlic, chopped
3 dry red chillies, torn into pieces
1 tsp turmeric powder
2 tsp coriander powder
1 tsp red chilli powder
4 tsp water

Ground to a fine paste:
½ medium-sized, fresh coconut, grated
¾ cup water

Tempering:

¾ tbsp oil
1 tsp mustard seeds
1 dry red chilli, torn into pieces
6 shallots, chopped
5 curry leaves
½ tsp fenugreek powder (methi)

- Clean sardines, remove heads, cut into 5-cm pieces, wash and drain well.
- Combine sardines, mango, onion, green chillies, ginger, curry leaves, salt, oil and spice paste in a pan.
- Stir in 1 cup water and place pan over high heat. Bring to boil, lower heat and cook for about 10 minutes.
- Mix in coconut paste and continue to cook over low heat till gravy thickens.
- Heat oil for tempering in a small pan and sprinkle in mustard seeds. When they start sputtering, add red chilli, shallots, and curry leaves. Fry till fragrant and remove from heat. Sprinkle in fenugreek powder and pour contents of pan into curry.
- Mix gently and serve.

VATTICHA MATHI KARI
Spicy Sardine Curry

Serves: 6

500 gms sardines
1 tbsp + 1 tbsp oil
1 medium-sized onion, chopped
4 cloves garlic, chopped
3-cm piece ginger, chopped
1 stalk curry leaves
½ tsp turmeric powder
3 petals cambodge, torn into pieces
1 tsp salt

Ground to a fine paste:
20 dry red chillies, torn into pieces
10 black peppercorns
2 tsp coriander seeds
½ tsp fenugreek seeds (methi)
¼ cup water

- Clean sardines, remove heads, wash and cut into 5-cm pieces.
- Heat 1 tbsp oil in a pan, add onion, garlic, ginger, curry leaves and turmeric, and fry till onion turns translucent.
- Mix in spice paste, fry for 2 minutes longer and remove from heat. Divide onion mixture, sardines and cambodge into 3-4 portions.
- Place a large shallow pan over heat and pour in 1 tbsp oil. Place a layer of sardines followed by a layer of onion mixture. Sprinkle a portion of cambodge over this. Repeat layering and pour in enough water to just

cover fish and onion mixture.
- Bring to boil, sprinkle in salt, lower heat and simmer till gravy turns dry.
- Serve with rice or kappa puzhukku.

NADAN MATHI KARI
Country-style Sardine Curry

Serves: 6

25 sardines
4 green chillies, slit
3 petals cambodge, torn into pieces and soaked in 1 cup water
1 tsp salt
½ tbsp + 1 tbsp oil
1 stalk curry leaves

Ground to a fine paste:
10 dry red chillies, torn into pieces
1 tsp coriander seeds
8 shallots, chopped
1 stalk curry leaves
¼ cup water

- Clean sardines, remove heads, cut into 5-cm pieces and wash.
- Combine sardines, green chillies, cambodge with its soaking liquid, salt, ½ tbsp oil and spice paste in a pan. Mix well and cook over low heat till fish is tender and gravy thickens.
- Stir in remaining oil and curry leaves, and remove from heat.
- Serve with rice or kappa puzhukku.

MEEN VARATHATHU – I
Fish-fry

Serves: 4

500 gms fish
Juice of 4 limes
1 cup oil

Ground to a fine paste:

4 shallots, chopped
4 green chillies, chopped
2 cloves garlic, chopped
3-cm piece ginger, chopped
1 stalk curry leaves
½ tsp salt
4 tsp water

Garnish:

3 medium-sized onions, chopped
3 medium-sized tomatoes, chopped
½ tsp red chilli powder
2 green chillies, slit
1 sprig coriander leaves, chopped
1 tsp coconut oil
½ tsp salt

- Clean fish, cut into 3-cm pieces, wash and drain.
- Mix lime juice with spice paste, rub into fish and marinate for 20 minutes.
- Heat oil in a kadhai and deep fry fish till cooked through and brown. Drain and arrange on a platter.
- Combine ingredients for garnish and scatter over fish.

MEEN VARATHATHU – II
Fish-fry

Serves: 4

500 gms fish
1 cup oil

Ground to a fine paste:
3-cm piece ginger, chopped
4 tsp red chilli powder
1 tsp coriander powder
½ tsp turmeric powder
½ tsp fenugreek seeds
1 tbsp white vinegar
1 tsp salt
4 tsp water

- Clean fish, cut into 3-cm pieces, wash and drain.
- Rub spice-paste into fish and marinate for an hour.
- Heat oil in a kadhai and deep fry fish till cooked through and brown.

Variation: Prawns can be fried in the same way.

THENGA CHERTHA MEEN VARATHATHU
Fried Fish with Coconut

Serves: 4

500 gms fish (pearl spot/pomfret)
½ cup oil

Coconut-spice paste:
½ cup grated fresh coconut
12 shallots, chopped
10 dry red chillies, torn into pieces
Juice of 1 lime
½ tsp turmeric powder
1 tsp salt

- Clean fish, keep whole with head and wash thoroughly.
- Place coconut, shallots and red chillies for coconut-spice paste in a pan over low heat and roast till coconut turns brown.
- Cool and add lime juice, turmeric and salt.
- Grind to a fine paste with ½ cup water.
- Rub paste over fish, stuff with remaining paste and marinate for an hour.
- Heat oil in a frying pan and shallow fry fish on both sides till cooked through and brown.
- Place fish in a platter and pour contents of frying pan over it.

Variation: Prawns can be fried in the same way.

MEEN PEERA
Shredded Fish with Coconut

Serves: 8

A Christian dish.

The peera style of cooking fish corresponds to the thoran method used in preparing vegetables.

500 gms fish fillet
4 green chillies, slit
3-cm piece ginger, chopped
3 petals cambodge, torn into pieces
1 tsp salt

Ground to a coarse paste:
1 medium-sized, fresh coconut, grated
4 shallots, chopped
2 cloves garlic, chopped
2 tsp coriander powder
2 tsp red chilli powder
½ tsp cumin seeds
1 tsp turmeric powder

Tempering:
1½ tbsp coconut oil
1 stalk curry leaves

- Clean fish, wash and chop extremely fine.
- Place fish, green chillies, ginger, cambodge, salt and coconut paste with scant ½ cup water in a pan and bring to boil.
- Lower heat, cover pan and cook for 10 minutes till no water remains.

155

- Heat oil for tempering in a small pan and add curry leaves. Fry for a few moments and pour contents of pan into fish. Mix well and serve.

MEEN MUTTA THORAN
Fish Roe with Coconut

Serves: 4

A Christian dish.

250 gms fish roe
½ medium-sized, fresh coconut, grated
5 green chillies, chopped
10 shallots, chopped
3-cm piece ginger, chopped
1 stalk curry leaves
½ tsp salt
1½ tbsp oil

- Wash roe thoroughly, remove membrane and chop fine.
- Combine roe with ¼ cup water and beat well. Add remaining ingredients except oil and mix well.
- Heat oil in a pan, add roe mixture and cook over low heat for 10-15 minutes, stirring continuously, till cooked.

Variation: Spread roe mixture on a tava or griddle and cook it like a pancake.

NADAN CHEMMEEN KARI
Country-style Prawn Curry

Serves: 8

500 gms medium-sized prawns
4 tsp red chilli powder
1 tsp coriander powder
3 green chillies, slit
8 shallots, chopped
3 petals cambodge, torn into pieces
3-cm piece ginger, chopped
½ tsp turmeric powder
¼ medium-sized, fresh coconut, chopped
1 tsp salt
1 stalk curry leaves
1½ tbsp oil

- Shell prawns, remove heads, devein and wash.
- Place all ingredients except curry leaves and oil, in a pan with ¾ cup water, and cook over low heat till prawns are cooked and gravy thickens.
- Mix in curry leaves and oil, and remove from heat.

Variation: Sun-dried prawns can be substituted for fresh prawns. Soak them in water for 30 minutes before use.

CHEMMEEN MAPAS
Prawn Curry with Coconut Milk

Serves: 4

A Christian dish.

250 gms prawns
1 tbsp oil
1 tsp mustard seeds
A pinch of fenugreek seeds
1 medium-sized onion, sliced
4 green chillies, slit
12 cloves garlic, chopped
5-cm piece ginger, sliced
2 walnut-sized balls of seedless tamarind soaked in ⅔ cup water
½ tsp salt
¾ cup coconut milk (1st extract; see p. 20)

Mixed together:

2 tsp coriander powder
½ tsp red chilli powder
1 tbsp water

- Shell prawns, remove heads, devein and wash.
- Heat oil in a pan and sprinkle in mustard seeds. When they start sputtering, add fenugreek, onion, green chillies, garlic and ginger, and fry till onion turns translucent.
- Mix in spice paste and fry for 2 minutes.
- Extract tamarind pulp and add with salt. Mix well and bring to boil.
- Add prawns and cook till prawns are half done.
- Pour in coconut milk, mix well, bring to boil and remove from heat.
- Serve with appam, idiappam, pathiri or puttu.

KASUANDIPARIPPU CHERTHA
CHEMMEEN KARI
Prawn Curry with Cashewnuts

Serves: 4

500 gms prawns
2 tbsp oil
4 medium-sized onions, chopped
2 medium-sized tomatoes, chopped
100 gms broken, unsalted cashewnuts
½ tsp red chilli powder
½ tsp black pepper powder
½ tsp turmeric powder
1 tsp salt
2 green chillies, slit
2 tsp white vinegar

Coconut paste:

2 tsp oil
½ medium-sized, fresh coconut, grated

Ground to a coarse paste:

3-cm piece ginger, chopped
3 cloves garlic, chopped

- Shell prawns, remove heads, devein and wash.
- Heat oil for coconut paste in a frying pan and fry till coconut turns brown. Cool and grind to a fine paste with ¾ cup water.
- Heat oil in a pan, add onions and fry till translucent.
- Stir in tomatoes and ginger-garlic paste, and cook for 2 minutes.
- Add prawns and cashewnuts, and fry for 5 minutes.

159

- Lower heat, sprinkle in spice powders and fry for a minute. Mix in salt and scant ½ cup water, and cook over low heat for 5 minutes. Add green chillies, vinegar and coconut paste, and cook till gravy thickens.
- Serve with appam, idiappam, pathiri or puttu.

CHEMMEEN ADA
Prawn Cutlets

Serves: 6

A Muslim dish.

500 gms medium-sized prawns
¼ cup rice flour
6 green chillies, chopped
10 shallots, chopped
3-cm piece ginger, chopped
2 stalks curry leaves, chopped
1 tsp salt
1 cup oil

- Shell prawns, remove heads, devein and wash.
- Place prawns in a pan with scant ½ cup water and cook over high heat till tender.
- Mash well and mix in remaining ingredients except oil. Roll mixture into walnut-sized balls and flatten to form cutlets.
- Heat oil in a kadhai and deep fry cutlets till golden.
- Serve with rice or porotta, or as a snack.

Variation: Boned fish can be substituted for prawns.

CHEMMEEN ULARTHIYATHU
Prawns with Potato and Coconut

Serves: 4

A Christian dish.

250 gms medium-sized prawns
2 tbsp oil
1 tsp mustard seeds
2 medium-sized onions, chopped
3 green chillies, slit
1 stalk curry leaves
¼ medium-sized, fresh coconut, chopped
2 tsp red chilli powder
½ tsp turmeric powder
1 tsp salt
3 medium-sized potatoes, cut into 1-cm pieces

- Shell prawns, remove heads, devein and wash.
- Heat oil in a pan and sprinkle in mustard seeds. When they start sputtering, add onions, green chillies, curry leaves and coconut, and fry, stirring constantly, till coconut turns brown.
- Stir in prawns, spice powders, salt, potatoes and scant ½ cup water. Cover pan and cook over low heat, stirring once in a while, till prawns and potatoes are cooked and gravy dries.
- Remove from heat and serve.

ERUVUM MADHURAVUM ULLA CHEMMEEN VARATHATHU
Sweet and Spicy Prawn-fry

Serves: 4

A Christian dish.

250 gms medium-sized or large prawns
1½ tbsp + 1½ tbsp oil
2 medium-sized onions, chopped
2 medium-sized tomatoes, chopped
3-cm piece ginger, chopped
2 tsp white vinegar
½ tsp turmeric powder
1 tsp salt
1 tsp sugar

Ground to a fine paste:
10 dry red chillies, seeded
6 cloves garlic, chopped
4 tsp water

- Shell prawns, remove heads, devein and wash.
- Heat 1½ tbsp oil in a pan, add onions and tomatoes, mix well, remove from pan and set aside.
- Pour remaining oil into pan and heat through. Add prawns, ginger, vinegar, turmeric and salt, and cook for 5 minutes.
- Reduce heat, add chilli-garlic paste and fry for 2 minutes.
- Add reserved onions and tomatoes, and fry till onions turn translucent.
- Stir in sugar, mix well and remove from heat.

PACHHATHAKKALI CHERTHA
CHEMMEEN THORAN
Mashed Prawns with Coconut and Green Tomatoes

Serves: 4

A Christian dish.

> 200 gms small or medium-sized prawns
> 3 medium-sized, green tomatoes, chopped
> 2 medium-sized onions, chopped
> 3-cm piece ginger, chopped
> 1 tsp salt

Ground to a coarse paste:
> ½ medium-sized, fresh coconut, grated
> 5 green chillies, chopped
> ½ tsp cumin seeds
> 1 tsp turmeric powder

Tempering:
> 1½ tbsp oil
> 1 tsp mustard seeds
> 1 tsp parboiled rice
> 3 dry red chillies, torn into pieces
> 3 shallots, chopped
> 2 stalks curry leaves

- Shell prawns, remove heads, devein and wash. Chop into very small pieces and mash on a grinding stone. (If prawns are very large boil lightly before chopping and mashing.)
- Mix prawns with tomatoes, onions, ginger and salt in a pan.

- Place pan over low heat and cook till water from prawns dries out.
- Add coconut-spice paste and continue to cook over low heat till it turns completely dry. Remove from heat.
- Heat oil for tempering in a small pan and sprinkle in mustard seeds. When they start sputtering, add remaining ingredients and fry till shallots turn brown.
- Pour contents of pan into prawns, mix well and serve.

THENGAPALUM PACHHA KAPPANGAYUM CHERTHA CHEMMEEN KARI
Prawn Curry with Unripe Papaya and Coconut Milk

Serves: 4

A Christian dish.

200 gms medium-sized prawns
150 gms unripe papaya
3 tbsp oil
2 medium-sized onions, chopped
3 medium-sized tomatoes, chopped
1 tsp salt
¾ cup coconut milk (1st extract; see p. 20)
1 tsp white vinegar

Ground to a fine paste:
2 cloves garlic, chopped
3-cm piece ginger, chopped
6 dry red chillies, torn into pieces
1 tbsp parboiled rice
2 tsp black pepper powder
½ tsp cumin seeds

½ tsp mustard seeds
½ tsp turmeric powder
2 tsp coriander powder
¼ cup water

- Shell prawns, remove heads, devein and wash.
- Peel papaya, remove seeds and cut into the same size as prawns.
- Heat oil in a pan, add onions and fry till translucent.
- Mix in spice paste and fry for a minute, stirring constantly.
- Add prawns and fry for 5 minutes, stirring occasionally.
- Mix in papaya, tomatoes and salt, and cook over low heat, stirring once in a while, till papaya is tender.
- Pour in coconut milk and vinegar, mix well and remove from heat. Serve with porotta or pathiri.

VARUTHARACHA NJANDU KARI
Crab Curry with Fried Coconut

Serves: 6

A Muslim dish.

500 gms crabmeat
1 tsp salt
3 shallots, chopped
4 green chillies, chopped
3-cm piece ginger, chopped
1 stalk curry leaves

Coconut paste:

1 tbsp oil
½ medium-sized coconut, grated
4 shallots, chopped
1 tsp black pepper powder
2 cloves garlic, chopped

Ground to a fine paste:

10 dry red chillies, torn into pieces
1½ tbsp coriander powder
1 tsp turmeric powder
4 tsp water

Tempering:

½ tbsp oil
3 shallots, chopped
1 stalk curry leaves

• Heat 1 tbsp oil for coconut paste in a frying pan, add coconut and shallots, and fry, stirring constantly, till coconut turns brown. Add pepper and garlic, and fry till the aroma of cooked garlic is released. Remove from heat, cool and grind to a fine paste with ¾ cup water.

- Clean crabmeat, wash and cut into 2-cm pieces.
- Place in a pan with salt and 1½ cups water, and cook over low heat for about 10 minutes.
- Add shallots, green chillies, ginger and curry leaves, and bring to boil.
- Stir in spice-paste and bring to boil again.
- Mix in coconut paste and cook over low heat till gravy thickens. Remove from heat.
- Heat oil for tempering in a small pan, add shallots and curry leaves and fry till shallots turn brown. Pour contents of pan into curry and mix well.
- Serve with rice, porotta, and pathiri.

NJANDU THORAN
Crab with Coconut

Serves: 6

A Muslim dish.

500 gms crabmeat
2 green chillies, slit
3-cm piece ginger, chopped
2 petals cambodge, torn into pieces
1 tsp salt
1 stalk curry leaves, crushed
1½ tbsp coconut oil

Ground to a coarse paste:
½ medium-sized, fresh coconut, grated
4 shallots, chopped
2 cloves garlic, chopped
1 tsp cumin seeds
3 tsp red chilli powder
1 tsp coriander powder
1 tsp turmeric powder

- Clean crabmeat and wash thoroughly.
- Combine crabmeat, green chillies, ginger, cambodge, salt, coconut paste and scant ½ cup water in a pan, and cook over low heat till water evaporates.
- Remove from heat, and add curry leaves and coconut oil. Mix well and serve.

NJANDU KARI – I
Crab Curry

Serves: 8

A Muslim dish.

1 kg crabs
3½ tbsp oil
1 tsp mustard seeds
1 tsp fenugreek seeds (methi)
2 medium-sized tomatoes, quartered
4 green chillies, chopped
5 cloves garlic, chopped
3-cm piece ginger, chopped
1 stalk curry leaves, chopped
2 lime-sized balls of seedless tamarind, soaked in 5 tbsp water
1 tsp salt

Mixed together:

3 tbsp red chilli powder
1 tbsp coriander powder
¼ tsp turmeric powder
¾ cup water

- Clean crabs and wash thoroughly.
- Heat oil in a pan and sprinkle in mustard seeds. When they start sputtering, add fenugreek and fry till fenugreek turns brown.
- Stir in spice paste and bring to boil.
- Add tomatoes, green chillies, garlic, ginger and curry leaves, and simmer for 5 minutes.
- Extract tamarind pulp, strain into pan and bring to boil. Mix in crabs and salt, cover pan and cook over low heat for 20 minutes.

169

NJANDU KARI – II
Crab Curry

Serves: 6

A Muslim dish.

500 gms crabmeat
1 tbsp oil
1 tsp mustard seeds
5 shallots, chopped
1 stalk curry leaves
4 tsp red chilli powder
1 tsp coriander powder
½ tsp turmeric powder
½ tsp black pepper powder
1 tsp salt

Coconut paste:

1 tbsp oil
½ medium-sized, fresh coconut, grated
10 shallots, chopped

- Clean crabmeat and wash.
- Heat 1 tbsp oil for coconut paste in a frying pan, add coconut and fry till brown, stirring constantly. Cool, mix with shallots and grind to a fine paste with ¾ cup water.
- Place crabmeat in a pan with ¾ cup water and cook for 10 minutes. Set aside.
- Heat 1 tbsp oil in a pan and sprinkle in mustard seeds. When they start sputtering, add shallots and curry leaves, and fry till shallots turn brown.
- Reduce heat, sprinkle in spice powders and fry for a

minute, stirring constantly.

- Add crabmeat with its stock, salt and ¾ cup water, and cook over low heat till it comes to boil.
- Mix in coconut paste, boil for 5 minutes and remove from heat. Serve with rice or porotta.

VARUTHARACHA KALLUMMEKAYA KARI
Mussel Curry with Fried Coconut

Serves: 6

A Muslim dish.

30 mussels
2 lime-sized balls of seedless tamarind soaked in 4 tsp water
or 1 unripe mango, sliced
1 tbsp red chilli powder
¼ tsp turmeric powder
1 tsp salt

Coconut paste:

1 tbsp oil
½ medium-sized, fresh coconut, grated
4 shallots, chopped
2½ tbsp coriander powder

Tempering:

1 tbsp oil
1 tsp mustard seeds
2 shallots, chopped
1 stalk curry leaves

- Wash and scrub mussels well. With a sharp knife, scrape off the poisonous beards and filaments at the joints of the shell.

- Place mussels in a pan with water to cover and boil for 30 minutes. Drain and prise open shells with the edge of a knife. Discard shells, rinse mussels in fresh water, drain and set aside.
- Heat 1 tbsp oil for coconut paste, add coconut and shallots, and fry, stirring constantly, till coconut turns brown.
- Reduce heat, add coriander powder and fry for 2 minutes longer. Remove from heat, cool and grind to a fine paste with ¾ cup water.
- Extract tamarind pulp (if used). Place tamarind or mango in a pan with mussels, spice powders, salt and 1½ cups water in a pan and cook over low heat for 10 minutes.
- Mix in coconut paste and bring to boil. Lower heat, cook till gravy thickens and remove from heat.
- Heat oil for tempering in a small pan and sprinkle in mustard seeds. When they start sputtering, add shallots and curry leaves, and fry till shallots turn brown.
- Pour contents of pan into curry, mix gently and serve with rice, porotta or pathiri.

Note: Discard any mussels that are not tightly shut.

KOONTHAL VARATIATHU
Stir-fried Squid

Serves: 4

A Muslim dish.

250 gms squid
2 tbsp oil
2 green chillies, slit
1 tsp salt

Ground to a coarse paste:
2 cloves garlic, chopped
2 tsp fennel seeds (badi saunf)
2 tsp red chilli powder
½ tsp turmeric powder

- Remove outer skin of squid, clean, wash thoroughly and cut into 3-cm pieces.
- Mix ground spices with 4 tbsp water.
- Heat oil in a pan over low heat and add squid, green chillies and spice paste. Mix well and cook, stirring occasionally, till water evaporates.
- Mix in salt and when completely dry, remove from heat.

UNAKKA MEEN KARI
Sun-dried Fish Curry

Serves: 4

250 gms sun-dried fish
2 tsp oil
4 cloves garlic, chopped
3 stalks curry leaves
½ tsp salt

Ground to a fine paste:
3 shallots, chopped
3-cm piece ginger, chopped
8 dry red chillies, torn into pieces
A walnut-sized ball of seedless tamarind
1 tsp turmeric powder
4 tsp water

- Wash fish and soak in water for an hour. Drain, dry and cut into 5-cm pieces.
- Rub spice paste into fish and marinate for an hour.
- Heat oil in a pan, add garlic and curry leaves, and fry till the aroma of cooked garlic is released.
- Pour in scant ½ cup water and stir in fish. Cook over low heat for 10 minutes.

Variation: Sun-dried prawns can be cooked in the same way. Soak in water for 30 minutes only.

UNAKKA MEEN VARATHATHU
Sun-dried Fish-fry

Serves: 6

500 gms sun-dried fish
4 tsp red chilli powder
½ tsp salt
½ tbsp + 2½ tbsp oil

- Wash fish and soak in water for an hour. Drain, dry and cut into 5-cm pieces.
- Mix chilli powder and salt with ½ tbsp oil, rub into fish and marinate for an hour.
- Heat remaining oil in a frying pan and shallow fry fish till crisp.

Variation: Sun-dried prawns can be cooked in the same way. Soak in water for 30 minutes only.

Biryani and cereals

The two principal wheat dishes in Kerala are porotta and alisa. Both are part of the Malayali Muslim culinary tradition. The latter is an important festive dish and stands apart in its uniqueness from the rest of Malayali cuisine.

On the other hand, the porotta has over the years travelled far from its home in north Kerala. It has now become the prime dish in most teashops, restaurants and fast food joints in Kerala. Outside the state, it graces the menus of most south Indian boutique restaurants, under the name Malabar porotta. All the other cereal preparations are made mostly with rice, which is not parboiled.

Malayalis usually consume these dishes for breakfast or as a snack. A meal, as understood both in households and restaurants, means a full course of parboiled rice, vegetables and a non-vegetarian dish depending upon personal preferences. The biryani is an exception to this.

IRACHI BIRYANI – I
Mutton Biryani with Coconut and Curd

Serves: 4

A Muslim dish.

500 gms mutton
1¼ cups basmati rice
½ tsp turmeric powder
1 tsp + 1 tsp salt
2½ tbsp + ½ tbsp ghee
2½ tbsp sultanas (kishmish)
2½ tbsp cashewnuts
2 medium-sized onions, chopped
3 medium-sized tomatoes, chopped
3 green chillies, slit
3 sprigs coriander leaves, chopped
2 stalks curry leaves
Scant ½ cup curd, whisked

Ground to a fine paste:
5 cloves garlic, chopped
5-cm piece ginger, chopped
5-cm stick cinnamon, broken into pieces
3 cloves
2 tsp fennel seeds (badi saunf)
2½ tsp red chilli powder
1 tsp coriander powder
1 tsp black pepper powder
1 tsp turmeric powder
¼ cup water

Ground to a fine paste:
½ medium-sized, fresh coconut, grated
¾ cup water

The Essential Kerala Cookbook

- Wash meat, drain and cut into 5-cm pieces.
- Place in a pressure cooker with scant ½ cup water and cook under pressure for 30 minutes.
- Wash rice and drain. Place in a pan with turmeric, 1 tsp salt and 3¾ cups lukewarm water, and mix gently. Bring to boil, lower heat, cover pan and cook till water is absorbed.
- Heat 2½ tbsp ghee in a pan, add sultanas and fry till they puff up. Remove from pan, drain and set aside. Add cashewnuts and fry till golden brown. Remove from pan, drain and set aside.
- Add onions to pan and fry till golden brown.
- Lower heat, stir in spice paste and fry for 5 minutes, stirring constantly.
- Add meat with its stock, 1 tsp salt and ¼ cup water, and simmer over low heat for 10 minutes.
- Mix in tomatoes, green chillies, coriander leaves, curry leaves, curd and coconut paste. Cook till gravy thickens and remove from heat.
- Grease a casserole with ½ tbsp ghee. Spread meat, rice and reserved sultanas and cashewnuts (in this order) in layers. Repeat layers, ensuring that the topmost layer is rice garnished with sultanas and cashewnuts.
- Cover tightly and place casserole on a tava or griddle over very low heat for 5 minutes. Remove from heat and serve with date and lime pickle.

Variation: Chicken can be substituted for mutton. In that case, there is no need to cook the chicken in advance.

181

IRACHI BIRYANI – II
Mutton Biryani with Egg

Serves: 4

A Muslim dish.

500 gms mutton
1 tsp black pepper powder
1 tsp + 1 tsp salt
½ cup ghee
2½ tbsp sultanas (kishmish)
2½ tbsp cashewnuts
3 medium-sized onions, sliced
1¼ cups basmati rice
5-cm stick cinnamon, broken into pieces
4 cloves
A pinch of saffron mixed with 1 tsp water
6 eggs, hard boiled and shelled

- Wash meat, drain and cut into 5-cm pieces.
- Place in a pressure cooker with pepper, 1 tsp salt and scant ½ cup water, and cook under pressure for 30 minutes.
- Heat ghee in a pan, add sultanas, cashewnuts and onions, and fry till onions turn translucent. Remove from ghee, drain and set aside.
- Wash rice, drain, add to pan and sauté for 10 minutes.
- Mix in 1 tsp salt and 3¾ cups lukewarm water. Bring to boil, lower heat, cover pan and cook till water is absorbed.
- Add meat with its stock, whole spices, saffron water, hard boiled eggs and reserved sultanas, cashewnuts and onions. Mix gently, taking care not to break the eggs.

- Cover pan and place over very low heat for 20 minutes.
- Serve with date and lime pickle.

Variation: Chicken can be substituted for mutton. In that case, there is no need to cook the chicken in advance.

MEEN BIRYANI
Fish Biryani

Serves: 6

A Muslim dish.

500 gms fish fillet (seer fish)
2½ cups basmati rice
1 tbsp + ½ cup + ½ tbsp ghee
1 tsp + 1 tsp salt
½ tsp + 1½ tsp turmeric powder
2½ tbsp sultanas (kishmish)
2½ tbsp cashewnuts
3 medium-sized onions, chopped
2 tsp red chilli powder
1 tsp coriander powder
5-cm stick cinnamon, broken into pieces
4 cloves
3 medium-sized tomatoes, chopped
Scant ½ cup curd, whisked

Marinade:

1 cup lime juice
½ tsp turmeric powder

- Wash fish and cut into 5-cm pieces.
- Combine ingredients for marinade, rub into fish and

marinate for 30 minutes.

- Wash rice and drain.
- Heat 1 tbsp ghee in a pan, add rice and sauté for 10 minutes. Add 1 tsp salt, ½ tsp turmeric and 1½ litres lukewarm water, and mix gently. Bring to boil, lower heat, cover pan and cook till water is absorbed.
- Heat ½ cup ghee in a pan, add sultanas and fry till they puff up. Remove from pan, drain and set aside. Add cashewnuts and fry till golden brown. Remove from pan, drain and set aside.
- Add onions to pan and fry till golden brown.
- Lower heat, mix chilli powder, coriander powder and 1½ tsp turmeric with 4 tsp water, and add to pan along with whole spices. Fry for 2 minutes, stirring constantly.
- Add fish and 1 tsp salt, and sauté for 5 minutes.
- Pour in ½ cup water, bring to boil and mix in tomatoes and curd. Lower heat and cook till gravy thickens.
- Grease a heavy-based pan with ½ tbsp ghee and spread fish, rice and reserved sultanas and cashewnuts (in this order) in layers. Repeat layers, ensuring that the topmost layer is rice garnished with sultanas and cashewnuts.
- Cover pan and place on a tava or griddle over very low heat for 5 minutes.
- Serve with date and lime pickle.

Variation: Large-sized prawns can be substituted for fish.

NEYCHHORU
Ghee Rice

Serves: 4

This pulao is typical to Malayali Muslims. It is customarily served by the bride's family on the eve of the wedding.

2½ cups basmati rice
3 tbsp ghee
2½ tbsp sultanas (kishmish)
2½ tbsp cashewnuts
4 medium-sized onions, chopped
5-cm stick cinnamon, broken into pieces
5 cloves
20 black peppercorns
1 tsp salt
A pinch of saffron dissolved in 2 tsp milk

- Wash rice and drain.
- Heat ghee in a pan, add sultanas and fry till they puff up. Remove from pan, drain and set aside. Add cashewnuts and fry till golden brown. Remove from pan, drain and set aside.
- Add onions and whole spices to pan and fry till onions turn translucent. Remove from pan, drain and set aside.
- Add rice to pan and sauté for 10 minutes.
- Mix in salt and 1 litre water, bring to boil, lower heat, cover pan and cook till water is absorbed.
- Carefully mix in reserved sultanas, cashewnuts, onions and whole spices.
- Sprinkle saffron-flavoured milk, mix gently and serve with a meat or fish curry.

185

THENGACHORU
Coconut Rice

Serves: 4

A Muslim dish.

2 cups basmati rice
2 tbsp ghee
1 medium-sized onion, sliced
3 cloves
5-cm stick cinnamon, broken into pieces
2 white cardamoms
1 medium-sized, fresh coconut, grated
2½ cups coconut milk (1st extract; see p. 20)
1 tsp salt

Ground to a fine paste:
2 tsp coriander powder
1 tsp turmeric powder
2 tsp fennel seeds (badi saunf)
4 tsp water

- Wash rice and drain.
- Heat ghee in a pan, add onion and fry till translucent.
- Toss in whole spices and fry for a minute till fragrant.
- Stir in coconut and spice paste, and fry for 5 minutes, stirring constantly.
- Pour in coconut milk and 1½ cups water. Add salt and bring to boil.
- Stir in rice, bring to boil, lower heat, cover pan and cook till water is absorbed.
- Serve with a pickle and pappadum.

CHEERACHORU
Rice with Amaranthus and Coconut

Serves: 4

Scant 1 cup basmati rice
250 gms amaranthus (cholai)
½ tsp salt
½ medium-sized, fresh coconut, grated

- Wash rice and drain.
- Wash amaranthus thoroughly and chop very fine.
- Place 2¼ cups water in a pan and bring to boil. Add rice, amaranthus and salt, and bring to boil again. Lower heat, cover pan and cook till water is absorbed.
- Mix in coconut and serve with a pickle and pappadum.

APPAM
Rice Pancakes with Coconut Milk

Serves: 4

A Christian dish.

Traditionally toddy was used to make appam. They are also called vellappam (white appam) and palappam (milk appam) denoting its colour and the use of coconut milk, respectively.

You will need an appachatti to prepare the appam.

1¼ cups rice
A pinch of dry yeast
½ tsp + ½ tsp sugar

½ cup cooked rice
A pinch of cumin powder
1½ cups coconut milk (1st extract; see p. 20)
½ tsp salt
1½ tbsp oil

- Wash rice and soak in water for 3 hours.
- Mix yeast with ½ tsp sugar and 2 tbsp lukewarm water, and set aside to ferment for an hour.
- Drain soaked rice and grind with cooked rice, cumin and yeast to a very fine paste with ¾ cup water. Add another 2 tbsp water if required.
- Pour in coconut milk, mix gently and set aside for a further 8 hours.
- Add salt and ½ tsp sugar just before cooking appam. (The quantity of sugar can be increased at this stage if you want the appam to taste sweet.)
- Coat an appachatti with oil and heat it. Pour in a ladle of batter. Tilt and rotate the appachatti so that the batter spreads all around. Cover and cook over low heat for 3 minutes.
- Serve with chicken, mutton or vegetable stew; prawn or fish moily; sweetened milk or coconut milk.

Note: If toddy is available use 1 cup toddy instead of dry yeast and reduce coconut milk to ¾ cup.

Another substitute for dry yeast is to mix 1 tsp sugar with coconut water, keep it near a source of heat, and use it on the fourth day.

IDIAPPAM
Rice String Hoppers

Serves: 6

South Indian shops generally sell the idiappam press (sevanazhi, or sevian machine) which is needed for making idiappam. However, you can make do with a potato ricer.

500 gms sifted rice flour (sift through a fine-meshed sieve and use only the finest flour)
½ tsp salt
½ medium-sized, fresh coconut, grated

- Mix rice flour with salt and 1½ cups hot water, and knead to make a dough. Fill an idiappam press with dough and press it out onto a lightly oiled idli mould.
- While pressing out the dough, move the press using a circular motion so that the strands fall in a circular pattern.
- As the dough emerges from the mould sprinkle a spoonful of coconut over it.
- Steam in a pressure cooker for 10 minutes without using the weight or pressure lock.
- Serve with mutton, chicken or vegetable stew; fish or prawn moily; sweetened milk or coconut milk.

Variation: To make sweetened idiappam mix 3 tsp sugar to the grated coconut before sprinkling it on the dough.

189

PUTTU
Steamed Rice with Coconut

Serves: 6

Puttu is probably the most common breakfast food in
Kerala's roadside teashops.

You will need a puttukutti, which is available in South
Indian stores, to prepare this.

2½ cups rice flour
½ tsp salt
½ medium-sized, fresh coconut, grated

- Mix rice flour, salt, ¾ cup water and a handful of
  coconut till rice flour is thoroughly soaked and smooth.
- Put a 3-cm layer of grated coconut at the base of a
  puttukutti and cover with a 6-cm layer of rice flour.
  Repeat layering till puttukutti is full.
- Fit puttukutti onto the metal utensil holding warm
  water. Raise heat and steam for 10 minutes.
- Serve with Bengal gram curry, or potato or chicken
  mapas, and pappadum.

Note: Puttu can also be eaten with ripe bananas. Generally,
the sweet-sour variety called palayankodan is preferred.

PATHIRI
Unleavened Rice Bread

Serves: 6

A Muslim dish.

Though pathiri are prepared in various ways the basic recipe is the one given below. They are usually eaten with meat, chicken or drumstick leaf curry.

1½ cups coconut milk (1st extract; see p. 20)
2½ cups sifted rice flour + extra for dusting (sift through a fine-meshed sieve and use only the finest flour)
½ tsp salt

- Place coconut milk in a pan and bring to boil. Mix in rice flour a little at a time. Add salt and keep stirring till it forms a dough.
- Cool and pinch off lime-sized balls of dough. Dust with rice flour and roll into thin, 10-cm round pathiri.
- Heat a tava or griddle and roast pathiri on both sides for about 2-5 minutes, taking care that they do not colour. They should remain white.

Variation: **Cheriya Ulliyum Thengayum Chertha Pathiri (Unleavened Rice Bread with Shallots and Coconut):** Prepare pathiri with water instead of coconut milk. Dip 3 sets of cooked pathiri in a finely ground paste made with ½ fresh coconut, 1 shallot and ¾ cup water.

PUZHUNGU PATHIRI
Unleavened Rice Bread Stuffed with Fish

Serves: 8

500 gms fish fillet (seer fish)
2 tsp red chilli powder
1 tsp turmeric powder
½ tsp salt
¾ cup + ¼ cup oil
1 medium-sized onion, chopped
4 green chillies, chopped
Rice flour for dusting

Rice dough:

1 kg parboiled rice
1 medium-sized, fresh coconut, grated
6 shallots, chopped
A pinch of cumin seeds
1½ cups water

Ground to a fine paste:

½ medium-sized, fresh coconut, grated
½ tsp red chilli powder
4 shallots, chopped
1 stalk curry leaves
½ tsp salt
¾ cup water

- Wash rice and soak in hot water for 8 hours.
- Hang rice in a muslin cloth for 2 hours to drain. Grind with remaining ingredients for rice dough.
- Wash fish and cut into 3-cm pieces.
- Combine spice powders with salt and coat fish with mixture.

- Heat ¾ cup oil in a frying pan and fry fish for about 5 minutes, till cooked through. Drain fish and mash lightly.
- Heat ¼ cup oil in a pan, add onion and fry till translucent. Add green chillies and fry for 5 minutes.
- Stir in coconut-spice paste and scant ½ cup water, and cook, stirring constantly, for about 5 minutes till you get the aroma of cooked coconut.
- Mix in fish and sauté for 5 minutes further.
- Pinch off lime-sized balls of rice dough, dust with rice flour and roll into thin, 10-cm round pathiri.
- Spread fish over half the pathiri and seal them with the rest. Steam for 10-15 minutes.
- Traditionally this is served with drumstick leaf curry.

THENGA CHERTHA PATHIRI
Unleavened Rice Bread with Coconut

Serves: 6

2½ cups parboiled rice
½ medium-sized, fresh coconut, grated
4 shallots, chopped
A pinch of cumin seeds
1 tsp salt
3 tbsp ghee
Rice flour for dusting

- Wash rice and soak in warm water for 8 hours.
- Drain rice and grind to a thick dough with coconut, shallots, cumin and ¾ cup water. Mix in salt.
- Heat a tava or griddle, spread a little ghee on it. Spread a ladle of dough on tava and cook on both sides till golden brown.

Variation: **Ney Pathiri (Unleavened Rice Bread with Ghee):** Pour ½ ladle of dough into hot ghee and deep fry till golden brown.

ALISA
Chicken and Wheat Porridge

Serves: 6

A Muslim dish which has some resemblance to the North African couscous. It is prepared with white or off white coloured wheat, but the regular wheat can also be used.

500 gms white wheat
250 gms boneless chicken
2 medium-sized onions, chopped
5-cm stick cinnamon, broken into pieces
1½ tsp salt
4 tbsp + 6 tbsp ghee
1 heaped tbsp sultanas (kishmish)
1 heaped tbsp cashewnuts
10 shallots, chopped

- Wash wheat and chicken, and drain. Cut chicken into 1-cm pieces.
- Place wheat, chicken, onions, cinnamon, salt, 4 tbsp ghee and 5 litres water in a heavy-based pan and cook, stirring frequently, for about 40 minutes till wheat is well cooked and soft, and water has evaporated. Transfer to a wide platter.
- Heat 6 tbsp ghee in a pan, add sultanas and fry till they puff up. Remove from pan, drain and set aside. Add cashewnuts and fry till golden brown. Remove from pan, drain and set aside. Add shallots to pan and fry till brown.
- Make a shallow depression in the centre of the alisa and pour in the ghee and fried shallots. Garnish with reserved sultanas and cashewnuts.
- Serve the alisa with sugar sprinkled on it.

POROTTA

Serves: 6

4 cups plain flour (maida)
½ tsp salt
A pinch of baking powder
1 tsp sugar
1 egg, beaten
1½ cups oil

- Sift flour with salt and baking powder. Mix in sugar.
- Add egg and 2 tbsp oil, and knead well with 1½ cups water to make a dough.
- Cover dough with an oiled damp cloth for 2 hours.
- Shape dough into orange-sized balls. Coat with oil and cover with a damp cloth for another hour.
- Oil a board and beat each dough ball on the board stretching and folding it repeatedly for at least 10 minutes. Apply oil at every stage. Finally, pull the ball into a 10-15-cm long, finger-thick shape. Coil it around itself and set aside for 15 minutes.
- Place each coil on a hot tava or griddle and flatten it with your hand to a disc 10-12 cm in diameter. Cook on both sides till brown.
- When 3-4 porotta are cooked, put them vertically together and hit from both sides with your palms. This gives them their characteristic loose and flaky look.

Pickles and chutneys

The Malayali has a whole array of pickles, chutneys and chutney powders—both vegetarian and non-vegetarian—for daily use. Some of them require skill and time. Others can be made easily and quickly and for these reasons they are served at feasts. The non-vegetarian pickles are typical to Malayali Christian and Muslim cuisine. They are called achar, while the vegetarian pickles are called kari. Achar is of Persian/Arabic origin and perhaps its usage in Kerala indicates that the art of making non-vegetarian pickles came through the Arabian Sea trade.

ARACHUKALAKKI
Coconut Chutney

Makes: 2 cups

1½ tbsp oil
1 tsp mustard seeds
1 tsp husked black beans (urad dal) – optional
2 shallots, chopped
1 stalk curry leaves
½ tsp salt

Ground to a fine paste:
½ medium-sized, fresh coconut, grated
4 green chillies, chopped or 6 dry red chillies torn into pieces
2 shallots, chopped
3-cm piece ginger, chopped
¾ cup water

- Heat oil in a pan and sprinkle in mustard seeds. When they start sputtering, add dal (if used), shallots and curry leaves, and fry till shallots turn brown.
- Mix ½ cup water and salt into ground coconut paste and stir in. Bring to boil and cook for a minute.
- Remove from heat and serve with idli, dosai or vada.

VARUTHA THENGA CHAMMANTHI
Browned Coconut Chutney

Makes: 250 gms

½ medium-sized, fresh coconut, grated
6 dry red chillies, torn into pieces or green chillies
1-cm piece ginger, chopped
2 shallots, chopped
1 stalk curry leaves
A walnut-sized piece of seedless tamarind or small unripe mango
1 tsp salt
¼ cup water

- Place coconut in a pan over low heat and cook till brown.
- Mix all ingredients together and grind to a coarse paste.

CHORUKKA CHERTHA THENGA CHAMMANTHI
Coconut Chutney with Vinegar

Makes: 200 gms

This chutney is usually served at the feast to celebrate Id.

½ medium-sized, fresh coconut, grated
6 green chillies, chopped
4 shallots, chopped
2 cloves garlic, chopped
1 tsp salt
1 tbsp white vinegar

- Mix all ingredients together and grind to a coarse paste.

VELLICHENNA CHERTA INJI CHAMMANTHI
Ginger Chutney with Coconut Oil

Makes: 75 gms

7½-cm piece ginger, chopped
6 dry red chillies, torn into pieces
4 shallots, chopped
A walnut-sized ball of seedless tamarind
1 stalk curry leaves
½ tsp salt
3 tsp coconut oil

- Mix all ingredients together except oil and grind to a coarse paste.
- Mix in oil.

INJITHAIRU – I
Curd and Ginger Chutney

Makes: ½ cup

Served at feasts

½ cup curd (not sour), whisked
4 green chillies, chopped
3-cm piece ginger, chopped
½ tsp salt

- Mix together all ingredients and serve.

INJITHAIRU – II
Curd and Ginger Chutney with Coconut

Makes: ¾ cup

5-cm piece ginger, ground
2 green chillies, ground
2 tbsp grated coconut, ground with 4 tbsp water
1 tsp salt
½ cup curd (not sour), whisked

Tempering:

2 tsp oil
½ tsp mustard seeds
¼ tsp cumin seeds
1 stalk curry leaves

- Mix together ginger, chillies, coconut, salt, curd and 2 tbsp water in a bowl.
- Heat oil for tempering in a small pan and sprinkle in mustard seeds. When they start sputtering, add cumin and curry leaves. Fry for a moment and pour contents of pan into bowl.
- Mix well and serve.

PULINJI
Tamarind and Ginger Chutney with Jaggery

Makes: 200 gms

Served at feasts.

2 walnut-sized balls of seedless tamarind, soaked in 5 tbsp water
1½ tbsp oil
1 tsp mustard seeds
½ tsp fenugreek powder (methi)
100 gms ginger, chopped
4 green chillies, chopped
2 dry red chillies, torn into pieces
1 stalk curry leaves
2 tsp red chilli powder
1 tsp salt
1 tsp powdered jaggery

- Extract tamarind pulp and set aside.
- Heat oil in a pan and sprinkle in mustard seeds and fenugreek. When mustard seeds start sputtering, add ginger, green chillies, red chillies and curry leaves, and fry for about 5 minutes, shaking the pan occasionally.
- Mix in chilli powder, salt and tamarind pulp, and boil till mixture thickens.
- Stir in jaggery and when it melts mix well and remove from heat. Allow to cool before serving.
- Use as soon as possible or refrigerate.

CHEMMEENUM PULIYUM CHERTHA CHAMMANTHI
Prawn and Tamarind Chutney

Makes: 300 gms

250 gms small prawns
1½ tbsp oil
2 medium-sized onions, chopped
3 cloves garlic, chopped
3-cm piece ginger, chopped
A walnut-sized ball of seedless tamarind soaked in 4 tsp water
1 tsp salt

- Shell prawns, remove heads, devein and wash.
- Heat oil in a pan, add onions and fry till brown. Remove from oil and set aside.
- Add garlic and ginger to pan and fry till the aroma of cooked garlic is released. Remove from oil and set aside.
- Extract tamarind pulp, strain and add to pan with prawns. Cook for till prawns are done, stirring constantly.
- Remove pan from heat, combine all ingredients, cool and grind to a paste.
- Serve as an accompaniment at a meal where rice is served.

Variation: Sun-dried prawns can be substituted for fresh prawns.

SHARKKARA CHERTH ADA MANGA
Sweet Mango Preserve

Makes: 600 gms

1 kg ripe, slightly sweet mangoes
50 gms salt
Syrup made from 100 gms jaggery (see p. 33)
25 gms red chilli powder
10 gms asafoetida powder (hing)

- Wash mangoes and dry thoroughly. Cut into 8 pieces each and discard seeds.
- Mix in salt and keep in the sun for 2 days.
- Place jaggery syrup in a pan over heat and boil till sticky.
- Mix in spice powders and add mangoes.
- Mix well and place pan in the sun, covered with a clean muslin cloth, till jaggery syrup dries. Stir once in a while.
- Store in an airtight jar and use after 3 days.

CHETHUMANGA KARI
Chopped Mango Pickle

Makes: 1¼ kg

Served at feasts.

1 kg unripe mangoes
100 gms salt
100 gms red chilli powder
10 gms asafoetida powder (hing)
2 tbsp sesame seed oil (til ka tael)

- Wash mangoes, dry thoroughly, chop into 1-cm cubes and discard seeds.
- Mix in salt and leave for 3 days.
- Add spice powders to mangoes and mix well.
- Heat oil in a pan till smoking. Cool and pour over mangoes.
- Store in airtight jars and use as soon as possible, or refrigerate.

KADUMANGA KARI – I
Oil-free Tender Mango Pickle

Makes: 600 gms

This pickle, rarely served at feasts, is also called 'kannimanga kari' in certain parts of Kerala. Most gourmets regard it as the queen of Malayali pickles. The problem is that not all tender mangoes yield the best pickle. The right type is the fruit of a very local variety of mango called chandrakaran. Frankly, it is easier to buy the pickle from a south Indian shop than to get this variety outside Kerala!

500 gms tender mangoes
50 gms salt
50 gms dry red chillies, seeded and powdered
50 gms mustard seeds, powdered
10 gms asafoetida powder (hing)

- Wash mangoes and dry thoroughly.
- Place layers of mangoes and salt in a dry stoneware pot. Keep tightly closed for 3 days and shake the pot once a day.
- Remove brine, place in a pan and bring to boil.
- Allow to cool and mix in spice powders.
- Pour over mangoes in the pot, cover with a piece of cloth dipped in sesame seed oil and close tightly. Seal with wax if possible.
- Use after 3 months.

Note: Chop mangoes and mix with chopped tomatoes, onions and cucumber for a tangy salad. Or cut mangoes into halves and serve with drinks as a spicy accompaniment. Use the seeds in both cases.

KADUMANGA KARI – II
Tender Mango Pickle with Fenugreek

Makes: 6 kg

5 kg tender mangoes
500 gms salt
100 gms fenugreek seeds (methi) dry roasted and ground
500 gms red chilli powder

- Wash mangoes and dry thoroughly. Slice off both ends of mango keeping seeds intact.
- Mix mangoes with salt in a dry stoneware pot and leave for 2 days.
- Sprinkle spice powders over mangoes, mix well and cover with a piece of cloth dipped in sesame seed oil. Close tightly and seal with wax if possible.
- Use after a month.

VARUTHA MANGA KARI
Mango Pickle

Makes: 1¼ kg

1 kg unripe mangoes
½ cup sesame seed oil (til ka tael)
100 gms red chilli powder
20 gms asafoetida powder (hing)
10 gms fenugreek powder
100 gms salt

- Wash mangoes, dry thoroughly, cut into 8 pieces each and discard seeds.
- Heat half the oil in a pan, add mangoes and fry for 5 minutes, stirring constantly.
- Heat remaining oil in a fresh pan till smoking. Cool and sprinkle in spice powders. Mix well and pour contents of pan into mangoes.
- Add salt and mix well. Bottle and use after 2 days.

ADA MANGA
Sun-dried Mango Pickle

Makes: 750 gms

1 kg unripe mangoes
2 tbsp sesame seed oil (til ka tael)
100 gms red chilli powder
20 gms asafoetida powder (hing)
100 gms salt

- Wash mangoes and dry thoroughly. Cut into 8 pieces each and discard seeds.
- Heat oil in a pan till smoking. Lower heat, sprinkle in spice powders and salt, and mix well. Add mangoes, mix well and remove from heat.
- Cool and place in an airtight jar in the sun for 4 days.
- Use after a month.

Variation: Rub mangoes with half the salt and place in the sun for 3 days. Continue as given above.

211

VELUTHULLIYUM CHORUKKAYUM CHERTHA MANGA KARI
Mango Pickle with Garlic and Vinegar

Makes: 700 gms

500 gms unripe mangoes
1 cup sesame seed oil (til ka tael)
1 tsp mustard seeds
1 tsp fenugreek seeds (methi)
5 cloves garlic, chopped
3-cm piece ginger, chopped
6 green chillies, chopped
1 stalk curry leaves
4 tsp salt
1½ tbsp white vinegar

Ground to a fine paste:

5 cloves garlic, chopped
3-cm piece ginger, chopped
6 tsp red chilli powder
1 tsp black pepper powder
1 tsp turmeric powder
½ tsp asafoetida powder (hing)
1½ tbsp vinegar

- Wash mangoes, dry thoroughly, cut into 1-cm pieces and discard seeds.
- Heat oil in a pan and sprinkle in mustard seeds. When they start sputtering, add fenugreek, garlic, ginger, green chillies and curry leaves, and fry till fragrant.
- Mix in salt and spice paste, and fry for 5 minutes.
- Stir in vinegar and remove from heat. Add mangoes, mix well and allow to cool.
- Bottle and refrigerate.

ULUVACHERTHA MANGA KARI
Mango Pickle with Fenugreek

Makes: 1¼ kg

1 kg unripe mangoes
100 gms salt
½ cup sesame seed oil (til ka tael)
100 gms red chilli powder
10 gms asafoetida powder (hing)
10 gms fenugreek powder

- Wash mangoes, dry thoroughly, cut into 3-cm long, 1-cm wide strips and discard seeds.
- Mix in salt and leave for 3 days.
- Heat oil in a pan till smoking. Cool and add chilli powder, asafoetida and fenugreek.
- Mix well and pour contents of pan over mangoes.
- Mix well, bottle and use after a month.

ENNAYILLATHA MANGA KARI
Oil-free Mango Pickle

Makes: 200 gms

1 large unripe mango
4 tsp salt

Ground to a fine paste:
1 tsp red chilli powder
1 tsp mustard seeds
½ tsp asafoetida powder (hing)

- Wash mangoes, dry thoroughly, cut into 1-cm pieces and discard seeds.
- Add ground paste and salt to mangoes.
- Mix well bottle and refrigerate.
- Use after a week.

NARANGA KARI
Lime Pickle

Makes: 1 kg

25 thin-skinned limes
10 green chillies, chopped
3-cm piece ginger, chopped
4 tsp salt
3½ tbsp sesame seed oil (til ka tael)
6 tsp red chilli powder

- Wash limes, dry thoroughly and cut into 8 pieces each.
- Mix limes, green chillies, ginger and salt, and keep in an airtight jar in direct sunlight for 3 days.
- Heat oil in a small pan till smoking. Cool and mix in chilli powder.
- Pour contents of pan over limes and mix well.
- Bottle and use after 7 days.

VARUTHA NARANGA KARI
Lime Pickle in Oil

Makes: 1 kg

25 thin-skinned limes
1 cup sesame seed oil (til ka tael)
1 tsp mustard seeds
1 tsp fenugreek seeds (methi)
3-cm piece ginger, chopped
4 cloves garlic, chopped
6 green chillies, chopped
2 stalks curry leaves
6 tsp salt

Ground to a fine paste:
3-cm piece ginger, chopped
6 cloves garlic, chopped
6 tsp red chilli powder
½ tsp asafoetida powder (hing)
1 tsp black pepper powder
1 tsp turmeric powder
1½ tbsp white vinegar

- Wash limes, dry thoroughly and cut into 8 pieces each.
- Heat 1½ tbsp oil in a frying pan and sauté limes till golden brown. Drain and set aside. Discard oil.
- Heat remaining oil in another pan and sprinkle in mustard seeds. When they start sputtering, add fenugreek, ginger, garlic, green chillies and curry leaves, and fry till the aroma of cooked garlic is released.
- Stir in spice paste and fry for 5 minutes, stirring frequently.
- Add salt and limes, mix well, remove from heat and allow to cool.
- Bottle and use after 3 days.

UNAKKA NARANGA KARI
Sun-dried Lime Pickle

Makes: 600 gms

25 thin-skinned limes
100 gms salt
2 tbsp sesame seed oil (til ka tael)
100 gms red chilli powder
25 gms asafoetida powder (hing)

- Wash limes, dry thoroughly and cut into 4 pieces each.
- Mix in salt and keep in the sun for 2 days.
- Heat oil in a pan till smoking, remove from heat and add chilli powder, asafoetida and limes. Mix well, cool, bottle and keep in the sun for 3 days.
- Stir once in a while and use after a month.

EENTHAPAZHAVUM NARANGAYUM
CHERTHA ACHAR
Date and Lime Pickle

Makes: ¾ kg

Malayali Muslims usually serve this pickle with biryani.

10 thin-skinned limes
1 heaped tbsp salt
250 gms seedless dates
5-cm piece ginger, chopped
3 cloves garlic, chopped
3½ cups white vinegar
3 tbsp red chilli powder

- Wash limes, dry thoroughly and cut into 8 pieces each.
- Rub limes with salt and keep in a stoneware pot for 3 days.
- Cut dates in half and add to limes with ginger, garlic and vinegar. Mix well and set aside for 24 hours.
- Mix in chilli powder, bottle and use after 2 weeks.

NELLIKA KARI
Amla Pickle

Makes: 1¼ kg

Nellika (in Malayalam) or amla (in Hindi) is the emblic gooseberry, also called the Indian hog plum. Its botanical name is *Emblica officinalis.*

A well-made amla pickle is highly prized by Malayali gourmets since it is a difficult achievement given the sour-sweet taste of the berry.

1 kg amla
½ cup + ½ cup sesame seed oil (til ka tael)
100 gms red chilli powder
20 gms asafoetida powder (hing)
10 gms powdered mustard seeds
100 gms salt

- Wash amla and dry thoroughly.
- Heat ½ cup oil in a frying pan and sauté amla till golden brown.
- Heat remaining oil in another pan, remove from heat and add spice powders and salt.
- Mix well and add amla. Mix again and store in an airtight jar. Use after 3 months.

PAVAKKA KARI
Bittergourd Pickle

Makes: 400 gms

250 gms bittergourds (karela)
100 gms red chilli powder
1 tsp turmeric powder
4 tsp salt
1 cup sesame seed oil (til ka tael)
2 tsp mustard seeds
2 tsp fenugreek powder (methi)
5 green chillies, slit
3-cm piece ginger, chopped
4 cloves garlic, chopped
A pinch of asafoetida powder (hing)
½ cup white vinegar

- Wash bittergourds and dry thoroughly. Slit open, remove seeds and cut into thin, 3-cm long slices.
- Mix half the chilli powder, turmeric and salt with bittergourds, and set aside for an hour.
- Heat oil in a kadhai, add bittergourds and deep fry till crisp. Remove from oil, drain and set aside.
- Sprinkle mustard seeds into kadhai. When they start sputtering, stir in fenugreek, green chillies, ginger and garlic, and fry for 5 minutes, stirring constantly.
- Combine asafoetida and remaining chilli powder, turmeric and salt, with vinegar and mix in. Fry for a minute and remove kadhai from heat.
- Mix in bittergourds, allow to cool and bottle.
- Use after 3 days.

IRACHI ACHAR
Meat Pickle

Makes: 500 gms

500 gms boneless meat
1 cup sesame seed oil (til ka tael)
6 green chillies, chopped
12 cloves garlic, chopped
4-cm piece ginger, chopped
2 stalks curry leaves
1½ tbsp white vinegar
1½ tsp salt

Marinade:

3 tsp red chilli powder
1 tsp turmeric powder
1½ tsp salt

Ground to a fine paste:

12 cloves garlic, chopped
4-cm piece ginger, chopped
3 tsp red chilli powder
1 tsp turmeric powder
1 tsp black pepper powder
1 tsp asafoetida powder (hing)

- Wash meat, pat dry and cut into 2-cm pieces.
- Combine ingredients for marinade, rub into meat and marinate for 30 minutes.
- Heat oil in a kadhai and deep fry meat till tender. Remove from oil, drain and set aside.
- Add green chillies, garlic, ginger and curry leaves to kadhai and fry for 5 minutes, stirring constantly.
- Mix in vinegar, salt, meat and ground spices, and remove from heat.
- Cool, bottle and store in the refrigerator.

221

MEEN/CHEMMEN ACHAR
Seafood Pickle

Makes: 500 gms

500 gms fish fillet (seer fish) or prawns
1¼ cups sesame seed oil (til ka tael)
1 tsp mustard seeds
5 green chillies, chopped
5-cm piece ginger, chopped
1 stalk curry leaves, chopped
1 tsp fenugreek seeds (methi)
10 cloves garlic, coarsely ground
4 tsp red chilli powder
1 tsp black pepper powder
½ tsp asafoetida powder (hing)
2 tsp salt
1 tbsp white vinegar

Marinade:

2 tsp red chilli powder
1 tsp turmeric powder
1 tsp salt
2 tbsp white vinegar

- Wash fish (if used), drain and cut into 2-cm pieces. Shell prawns (if used), remove heads, devein and wash.
- Combine ingredients for marinade, rub into seafood and marinate for 30 minutes.
- Heat oil in a kadhai, add seafood and fry for 5 minutes till brown. Drain and set aside.
- Sprinkle mustard seeds into oil. When they start sputtering, add green chillies, ginger, curry leaves and fenugreek, and fry for 5 minutes. Mix in remaining ingredients and remove from heat.
- Cool and store in an airtight jar in the refrigerator.

KALLUMMEKAYA ACHAR
Mussel Pickle

Makes: 750 gms

30 mussels
1 cup sesame seed oil (til ka tael)
1 tsp mustard seeds
50 gms green chillies, chopped
25 gms garlic, chopped
50 gms ginger, chopped

Marinade:

50 gms red chilli powder
½ tsp turmeric powder
3 tsp salt

Mixed to a paste:

100 gms red chilli powder
½ tsp turmeric powder
2¼ tbsp fenugreek powder (methi)
½ tbsp asafoetida powder (hing)
¾ cup white vinegar

- Wash and scrub mussels well. With a sharp knife, scrape off the poisonous beards and filaments at the joints of the shell. Wash again. Prise open shells with the edge of a knife. Rinse in fresh water and drain.
- Combine ingredients for marinade, mix in mussels and marinate for 30 minutes.
- Heat oil in a kadhai and deep fry mussels till golden brown. Remove from oil, drain and set aside.
- Sprinkle mustard seeds into oil. When they start sputtering, add green chillies, garlic and ginger, and fry for 5 minutes. Add spice paste and fry for a minute

more, stirring constantly.
- Mix in mussels, remove from heat and cool.
- Store in an airtight jar in the refrigerator.

Note: Discard any mussels that are not tightly shut.

THENGA CHAMMANTHI PODI
Coconut Chutney Powder

Makes: 250 gms

1 tsp coconut oil
1 medium-sized, fresh coconut, grated
10 shallots, chopped
12 dry red chillies, torn into pieces
3-cm piece ginger, chopped
2 stalks curry leaves
2 lime leaves, torn into pieces
10 black peppercorns
1 tsp coriander powder
A walnut-sized ball of seedless tamarind
A pinch of asafoetida powder (hing)
2 tsp salt

- Heat oil in a frying pan, add coconut, shallots and red chillies, and fry, stirring constantly, till coconut turns brown.
- Add ginger, curry leaves, lime leaves, peppercorns and coriander powder, and continue to fry till coriander powder releases its aroma.
- Cool and mix in tamarind, asafoetida and salt.
- Grind to a fine powder and store in a dry bottle.

UNAKKA MEEN CHAMANTHI PODI
Sun-dried Fish Chutney Powder with Coconut

Makes: 400 gms

200 gms sun-dried fish (anchovy)
4 tsp + 4 tsp oil
½ medium-sized, fresh coconut, grated
10 dry red chillies, torn into pieces
5 shallots, chopped
A walnut-sized ball of seedless tamarind
3-cm piece ginger, chopped
1 stalk curry leaves
1 tsp salt

- Wash fish and soak in water for an hour. Drain and dry thoroughly.
- Heat 4 tsp oil in a frying pan, add fish and fry till golden brown. Remove from pan and set aside.
- Add remaining oil to pan and heat through. Mix in remaining ingredients and fry, stirring constantly, till coconut turns brown.
- Remove pan from heat, mix in fish and cool.
- Grind to a coarse powder and serve as an accompaniment at a meal where rice is served.

Note: This chutney powder can be eaten dry or a little water can be added to make a thick paste.

Variation: Sun-dried prawns can be used in place of the fish. Soak them for 30 minutes only.

MULAGU KONDATTAM
Dried Chilli Fries

Makes: 250 gms

250 gms green chillies, kept whole, with stems intact
1½ cups curd, whisked
1 heaped tbsp salt

- Wash chillies, plunge into boiling water and remove immediately. Spread out on a tray, cover with a thin muslin cloth and keep in the sun for 2 days.
- Mix salt and curd in a bowl, add chillies and leave for 2 hours.
- Remove chillies from mixture and spread out on the tray again. Keep in the sun till chillies are completely dry. Store in a bottle.
- Deep fry chillies as required and serve as an accompaniment at a meal where rice is served.

PAVAKKA KONDATTAM
Dried Bittergourd Fries

Makes: 50 gms

250 gms bittergourds (karela)
6 tsp red chilli powder
1 tsp turmeric powder
2 tsp salt

- Wash bittergourds and dry thoroughly. Cut into thin round slices and remove seeds.
- Combine spice powders and salt, and rub into bittergourds.
- Spread out on a tray, cover with a thin muslin cloth, keep in the sun for 3 days till completely dry and bottle.
- Deep fry bittergourds as required and serve as an accompaniment at a meal where rice is served.

Sweets and savouries

Payasam, liquid dishes sweetened with either sugar or jaggery, occupy pride of place at all feasts. The sweetening agent is either sugar or jaggery. Sugar based payasam, as we know it today, cannot be older than the beginning of the nineteenth century when a modern industry producing white crystalline sugar was established in India. However, jaggery has always been here. Achaya says the English word 'jaggery' is derived from the Portuguese corruption 'xagara', 'jagara' and 'jagra' of the Malayalam word 'chakkara'. This word in turn comes from the Sanskrit 'sharkkara'. Currently, both the Malayalam and Sanskrit words have distinctively different meanings in Kerala. Chakkara commonly refers to palm jaggery and sharkkara to sugar cane jaggery. The first is rarely used in sweets. However, it is a sweetening agent in black coffee and its smoky flavour does enhance the taste.

Payasam have always been used as ritual offerings. While milk and sugar-based payasam are offered at Vaishnavite temples, in Shaivite and Devi temples jaggery-based payasam are the rule. In fact some temples are famous for the quality of the payasam which is prepared as prasadam or a ritual offering in the temple kitchens. Examples are the milk-based palpayasam at the Ambalapuzha Krishna temple and the jaggery-based neypayasam at the Chottanikara Devi temple.

While payasam come from the Namputhiri-Nair culinary tradition, Malayali Christian cuisine is noted for its cookies and steamed sweets and savouries. Malayali Muslim cuisine, on the other hand, creates imaginative egg dishes and has many variations of the halva. It makes use of steaming as well as baking.

PALADA PRADHAMAN
Steamed Rice Flake Dessert

Serves: 6

This is one of the two payasam served at a sadya. The quality of the palada pradhaman depends upon the quality of the ada. A well-made ada has a translucent look when cooked. This level of quality is not easy to achieve. While ready-to-use ada available at south Indian shops may not be of the best quality, they allow for ease of cooking. Before using soften them in boiling hot water.

500 gms ada (see p. 34)
½ cup ghee
100 gms sultanas (kishmish)
100 gms unsalted cashewnuts
2 litres milk
1 kg sugar
4 white cardamoms, powdered

- Soak ada in boiling hot water for 30 minutes to soften.
- Heat ghee in a pan, add sultanas and fry till they puff up. Remove from pan, drain and set aside. Add cashewnuts and fry till golden brown. Remove from pan, drain and set aside.
- Drain ada, add to pan and fry till golden.
- Stir in milk and sugar, bring to boil and continue to boil till milk turns slightly brown and has a thick flowing consistency.
- Mix in cardamom powder and reserved sultanas and cashewnuts, and remove from heat immediately.
- Serve hot.

KADALAPARIPPU PAYASAM
Bengal Gram Dessert

Serves: 6

A feast is incomplete unless a brown payasam (jaggery-based) is served after a white payasam like the palada pradhaman.

> 1 tbsp + 3 tbsp + 1 tbsp ghee
> 500 gms Bengal gram (chana dal)
> Syrup made from 500 gms jaggery (see p. 33)
> 6 cups coconut milk (3rd extract; see p. 20)
> 3 cups coconut milk (2nd extract)
> 2 cups coconut milk (1st extract)
> 6 white cardamoms, powdered
> ½ dry coconut (copra), cut into small wedges
> 2½ tbsp sultanas (kishmish)
> 2½ tbsp unsalted cashewnuts

- Heat 1 tbsp ghee in a pan, add dal and fry till golden brown.
- Pour in jaggery syrup and 2½ cups water. Mix well and cook till dal softens.
- Mash well, add 3 tbsp ghee and stir and cook till mixture has the consistency of a thick porridge.
- Stir in third extract of coconut milk. Bring to boil and continue boiling till it thickens slightly, stirring occasionally.
- Stir in second extract of coconut milk. Bring to boil and continue boiling till it thickens a little more, stirring occasionally.
- Stir in first extract of coconut milk and cardamom powder and remove from heat. The consistency should

233

be that of a thin porridge.
- Heat 1 tbsp ghee in a small frying pan and fry dry coconut till brown. Remove from pan, drain and set aside.
- Add sultanas to pan and fry till they puff up. Remove from pan, drain and set aside. Add cashewnuts and fry till golden brown. Remove from pan, drain and set aside.
- Add all fried ingredients with any ghee left in the pan to payasam. Mix well and serve hot.

Variation: Pre-boiled whole wheat can be used instead of Bengal gram. Add 4 mashed kadalipazham (a variety of banana) to enhance the flavour.

PAZHA PRADHAMAN
Ripe Plantain Dessert

Serves: 6

Served at feasts.

6 ripe plantains
¾ cup ghee
Syrup made from 700 gms jaggery (see p. 33)
6 cups coconut milk (3rd extract; see p. 20)
3 cups coconut milk (2nd extract)
2 cups coconut milk (1st extract)
4 white cardamoms, powdered

- Peel plantains, cut into 1-cm pieces and place in a pan with 2½ cups water. Place pan on heat and boil till it turns red, stirring occasionally.
- Add ghee, mix well and fry for 5 minutes, stirring constantly.
- Pour in jaggery syrup, mix well and cook, stirring till it has the consistency of a thick porridge.
- Stir in third extract of coconut milk. Bring to boil and continue boiling till it thickens slightly, stirring occasionally.
- Stir in second extract of coconut milk. Bring to boil and continue boiling till it thickens a little more, stirring occasionally.
- Stir in first extract of coconut milk and cardamom powder, and remove from heat. The consistency should be that of a thin porridge.
- Serve hot.

ARI PAYASAM
Red Rice Dessert

Serves: 6

Traditionally the rice used for this payasam was a local variety called adhikarazi nellu which has a red tinge. Since it was hand-milled without parboiling the bran improved the tone of the red tinge even further. South Indian shops sometime stock this rice. However, a passable payasam can also be made with ordinary rice.

250 gms red rice
4 litres milk
100 gms unsalted butter
2½ cups sugar

- Wash rice, drain and place in a pan with 1 litre milk and 2 litres water, and cook till half done.
- Add butter and cook, stirring constantly, for 5 minutes.
- Add sugar and keep stirring till dissolved.
- Stir in remaining milk and cook till it thickens, stirring occasionally. The consistency should be that of a thin porridge.
- Remove from heat and serve hot.

Note: You can cook the rice with 1 litre water in a pressure cooker for 15 minutes and continue as given. Add all the milk after dissolving sugar.

MAMPAZHAM CHERTHA RAVA PAYASAM
Semolina Dessert with Mango

Serves: 6

A Christian dish.

3 ripe table mangoes
1 cup semolina (sooji/rava)
2 tsp ghee
Syrup made from 250 gms jaggery (see p. 33)
2 tsp plain flour (maida)
½ cup sugar
4 cups coconut milk (1st extract; see p. 20)
2 cups milk (pre-boiled)
4 white cardamoms, powdered

- Peel mangoes and cut into 1-cm pieces.
- Place semolina in a pan with 1½ cups water and cook for 5 minutes till done.
- Add ghee, jaggery syrup and 1½ cups water, and bring to boil. Mix flour with 1 tbsp water, add to pan with sugar and mangoes, and bring to boil again.
- Add coconut milk and milk, bring to boil once more, and boil for 2 minutes.
- Stir in cardamom powder and remove from heat.
- Serve hot.

NEYPAYASAM
Rice and Ghee Dessert

Serves: 6

1 cup ghee
2½ tbsp sultanas (kishmish)
2½ tbsp unsalted, cashewnuts
200 gms red rice
Syrup made from 1½ kg jaggery (see p. 33)
1 litre coconut milk (1st extract; see p. 20)
50 gms sugar candy (misri)

- Heat 1 tbsp ghee in a pan, add sultanas and fry till they puff up. Remove from pan, drain and set aside. Add cashewnuts and fry till golden brown. Remove from pan, drain and set aside. Reserve ghee in pan and set aside.
- Wash rice, drain, place in a pan with 2½ cups water and cook till half done.
- Add jaggery syrup and remaining ghee, and fry, stirring constantly till completely dry.
- Mix in coconut milk, sugar candy and reserved sultanas, cashewnuts and ghee, and cook till payasam thickens. The consistency should be that of a thick porridge.
- Serve warm.

MADAKUSAN
Coconut Pancake

Serves: 8

A Christian dish.

> 4 cups plain flour (maida)
> ½ tsp salt
> 1 egg, beaten
> 1½ cups coconut milk (1st extract; see p. 20)
> ½ tbsp + 1½ tbsp sugar
> ½ medium-sized, fresh coconut, grated
> 4 white cardamoms, powdered
> 1½ tbsp ghee

- Sift flour with salt into a bowl, beat in egg, coconut milk and ½ tbsp sugar. Keep batter aside.
- Mix 1½ tbsp sugar with coconut and cardamom powder, and set aside.
- Heat a little ghee in a frying pan. Pour in a large ladleful of batter and spread it to make a pancake. Cook till golden brown at the base. Flip over and cook till golden brown on the other side.
- Place 1 tbsp coconut-sugar mixture on one side of pancake, fold and remove from heat.
- Continue making pancakes, adding ghee to pan as required, till all the batter is used up.
- Serve with honey or sugar syrup.

MADHURA KARI
Ripe Plantain and Rice Pudding

Serves: 6

A Muslim dish served at feasts.

500 gms parboiled rice
¼ tsp + ¼ tsp salt
1 banana leaf
1 litre coconut milk (1st extract; see p. 20)
5 ripe plantains
1 cup sugar
2 tbsp rice flour
5 white cardamoms, powdered

- Wash rice and soak in water for 5 hours. Drain and grind with ¾ cup water and ¼ tsp salt to a thick paste.
- Shape into small grape-sized balls, place on banana leaf and steam for 15 minutes. Allow to cool and sprinkle over cold water to separate the balls.
- Place coconut milk in a pan with ¼ tsp salt, add rice balls and cook for 5 minutes.
- Peel plantains and cut into 1-cm pieces.
- Add to pan and cook for about 10 minutes more, stirring occasionally.
- Add sugar, bring to boil and cook till it thickens to the consistency of a thin porridge.
- Mix rice flour with scant 1 cup water and add to pan with cardamom powder. Allow to boil and thicken further to the consistency of a thick porridge.
- Serve warm.

THARI KACHIYATHU
Semolina Pudding

Serves: 4

A Muslim dish, usually served after the fast is broken.

2 tbsp semolina (sooji/rava)
1 cup milk
½ cup sugar
1 tbsp ghee
2 shallots, chopped
2½ tbsp sultanas (kishmish)
2½ tbsp unsalted cashewnuts

- Boil scant ½ cup water in a pan, add semolina, and stir and cook for 10 minutes.
- Add milk and sugar, bring to boil and remove from heat.
- Heat ghee in a frying pan, add shallots, sultanas and cashewnuts, and fry till shallots turn brown.
- Remove from heat and pour contents of pan into semolina.
- Mix well and serve.

VALSAN
Steamed Rice and Plantain Sweet

Serves: 15

This dish is also known as ada in some parts of Kerala. It is the traditional early morning offering made to Mahabali when he makes his annual visit to Kerala on Thiruonam day, which marks the climax of the Onam festivities.

1 kg rice
1 tsp salt
Syrup made from 1 kg jaggery (see p. 33)
4 ripe plantains, peeled and chopped
1 medium-sized, fresh coconut, grated
15 banana leaves

- Wash rice and soak in water for 3 hours. Drain and grind to a thick paste with salt and 1½ cups water.
- Heat jaggery syrup in a pan and cook till thickened.
- Add plantains and coconut, mix well and cook till it dries completely to a thick paste.
- Clean banana leaves with a damp cloth on both sides, dry and pass over a live flame to make them pliable.
- Spread a large spoonful of rice paste on each banana leaf. On one half of the rice paste spread jaggery paste. Fold leaves from all sides to make a parcel so that the jaggery paste is covered by the rice paste.
- Steam for 15 minutes.
- Serve immediately.

UNNIAPPAM
Fried Banana and Rice Sweet

Serves: 12

Unniappam is often used as a ritual offering in temples dedicated to Krishna (generally represented as a child) in Kerala. The size of the unniappam are considerably smaller when made in temples. I have never understood whether this is a literal interpretation of the word unni, meaning child, or a measure of economy practised by temples!

The banana used for this dish is a local variety called palayankodan. It is short, yellow skinned and has a sweet-sour taste. Unniappam are made in a cast iron mould called an appakara. Each appakara generally has moulds to accommodate 4 unniappam.

150 gms ripe table bananas
Syrup made from 150 gms jaggery (see p. 33)
250 gms rice flour
1 tsp cumin powder
1 tsp ginger powder (saunth)
½ tsp salt
2½ cups oil

- Peel bananas and mash to a smooth paste. Add jaggery syrup, rice flour, cumin, ginger, salt and 2 tbsp water, and mix well to form a smooth batter.
- Heat an appam mould (appakara) and pour in oil. When oil reaches smoking point, pour 1 tbsp batter into each mould and deep fry.

KUMBILA APPAM
Steamed Jackfruit Cones

Serves: 12

A Christian dish.

15 vayana leaves
500 gms ripe jackfruit
250 gms rice flour
Syrup made from 250 gms jaggery (see p. 33)
6 white cardamoms, powdered
½ tsp cumin powder
½ tsp ginger powder (saunth)
1 medium-sized, fresh coconut, grated
½ tsp salt

- Wash and dry vayana leaves. Shape leaves into cones using toothpicks to secure them.
- Clean jackfruit, remove seeds and grind flesh to a fine paste.
- Mix jackfruit with remaining ingredients.
- Put 1 tbsp mixture into each vayana leaf cone. Arrange them upright in a steamer and steam for 10 minutes.

Note: The vayana (also called vazhana) tree is *Laurus cassis*. It belongs to the family of the bay leaf. Leaves of banana, jackfruit or cinnamon trees, or fresh bay leaves can be substituted for vayana leaves. However, they will not have the same aroma.

MADURAM CHERTHA NENTHRAKAYA
Unripe Plantain Dessert

Serves: 6

5 unripe plantains
1 cup oil
2½ cups sugar
1½ tbsp ghee
½ medium-sized, fresh coconut, grated
1 tsp rose-water

- Peel plantains, slit lengthwise and cut into 3-cm long, 1-cm thin slices.
- Heat oil in a frying pan and fry plantain slices till crisp and golden. Drain and set aside.
- Combine sugar with ½ cup water in a pan, place over moderate heat and stir till sugar dissolves. Bring to boil and boil to the soft-ball stage. (A little syrup poured into a cup of cold water forms a soft ball.)
- Stir in ghee and coconut, and cook till mixture thickens and becomes string-like.
- Add rose-water and plantains, and continue cooking and stirring till completely dry.
- Remove from heat and serve.

NENTHRAPAZHAM ADA
Plantain and Rice Dessert in Banana Leaves

Serves: 6

4 ripe plantains
250 gms rice flour
½ medium-sized, fresh coconut, grated
½ cup sugar
4 white cardamoms, powdered
10 banana leaves
1½ tbsp oil

- Steam plantains for 10 minutes, peel and mash.
- Add rice flour, coconut, sugar and cardamom powder, and knead to make a dough.
- Clean banana leaves with a damp cloth on both sides, dry and pass over a live flame to make them pliable. Cut into 20-cm pieces.
- Wet banana leaves and spread dough over them thinly with your fingers.
- Fold leaves to cover dough and make ada.
- Heat a tava or griddle and spread a little oil evenly over it.
- Place an ada on tava and roast on both sides till leaf turns brown.
- Remove from heat and serve with or without the banana leaf wrapping.

MUTTAMALA
Garland of Eggs

Serves: 8

This Muslim sweet dish resembles the Afghani abraysham kabaub except that while the latter uses the whole egg this dish is made with egg yolks. Use the egg whites to make pinjanathappam (next recipe).

Using a hole made in a coconut shell as a dropper is an obvious Malayali innovation.

½ coconut shell (with the 3 depressions)
2½ cups sugar
Yolks of 20 eggs

- Clean coconut shell and prise open one depression.
- Place sugar with 1½ litres water in a pan over moderate heat and stir till sugar dissolves. Bring to boil and keep it simmering over low heat.
- Beat yolks and strain through a clean piece of cloth.
- Bring sugar syrup to boil.
- Cover the hole in the coconut shell with your finger and pour egg yolk into shell. Hold shell over boiling sugar syrup, move your finger aside and allow yolk to drip into sugar syrup in a garland-like pattern. (It is this pattern which lends its name to the dish.)
- Cook for 2 minutes and remove yolk with a slotted spoon.
- Sprinkle a little water into the boiling sugar syrup, very carefully, and repeat till all the yolk is used up.
- Serve as it is or over pinjanathappam.

247

PINJANATHAPPAM
Steamed Egg White Dessert

Serves: 8

A Muslim dish.

You can use the egg white and the sugar syrup left over from making muttamala (previous recipe) to make pinjanathappam.

1 cup sugar
Whites of 20 eggs
1¼ cups plain flour (maida)
8 white cardamoms, powdered
1 tbsp ghee

- Place sugar with 3¼ cups water in a pan over moderate heat and stir till sugar dissolves. Bring to boil and boil till syrup reaches the thread stage. (A little syrup poured into a cup of cold water forms a thin thread.)
- Remove pan from heat and allow syrup to cool.
- Beat egg whites with sugar syrup, flour, cardamom powder and half the ghee.
- Coat a round dish with remaining ghee and pour in mixture. Place in an idli utensil or pressure cooker and steam for 20 minutes.
- Serve as it is or spread muttamala over it.

PAZHAM PORI
Plantain Fritters

Serves: 6

This sweet dish is standard fare in roadside tea-shops.

5 ripe plantains
1 cup plain flour (maida)
½ cup sugar
¼ tsp turmeric powder
A pinch of salt
2½ cups oil

- Peel plantains, slit lengthwise and cut into halves.
- Mix flour with ½ cup water to make a smooth batter. Mix in sugar, turmeric and salt.
- Heat oil in a kadhai, dip plantain slices in batter and deep fry till golden brown. Drain and serve hot.

NENTHRAPAZHAM CHERTHA MUTTA THORAN
Plantain and Egg Dessert

Serves: 4

A Muslim dish.

4 semi-ripe plantains
½ cup ghee
1 heaped tbsp sultanas (kishmish)
1 heaped tbsp unsalted cashewnuts
3 eggs, lightly beaten
4 white cardamoms, powdered
½ cup sugar

- Peel plantains and cut into 1-cm pieces.
- Heat ghee in a pan, add sultanas and fry till they puff up. Remove from pan, drain and set aside. Add cashewnuts and fry till golden brown. Remove from pan, drain and set aside.
- Add plantains to pan and sauté for 10 minutes.
- Add eggs, cardamom powder and sugar. Stir vigorously to scramble eggs, garnish with reserved sultanas and cashewnuts, and serve immediately.

UNNAKKAYA
Coconut-filled Plantain Fritters

Serves: 6

A Muslim dish.

Unnakkaya means the pod of the cotton tree and lends its name to this dish because of the similarity in shape of the sweet.

1 kg ripe plantains
½ cup sugar
½ medium-sized, fresh coconut, grated
5 eggs, well beaten
4 white cardamoms, powdered
1 cup oil

- Peel plantains and cut into 5-cm pieces.
- Steam plantains for 10 minutes and grind to a fine paste.
- Place sugar with 1 cup water in a pan over moderate heat and stir till sugar dissolves. Bring to boil and boil till syrup thickens.
- Add coconut and keep cooking and stirring till it dries.
- Add eggs and cardamom powder and continue to cook and stir till completely dry. Remove from heat and allow to cool.
- Shape plantain paste into small balls and flatten on your palm. Place 1 tsp coconut mixture in the centre and cover with plantain paste to form oval fritters.
- Heat oil in a kadhai and deep fry fritters till golden brown.
- Remove from oil, drain and serve warm.

NENTHRAPAZHAM NIRACHATHU
Coconut-filled Plantain Fritters

Serves: 8

½ cup sugar
½ medium-sized, fresh coconut, grated
5 eggs, lightly beaten
4 white cardamoms, powdered
1 kg semi-ripe plantains
Scant 1 cup plain flour (maida)
½ tsp salt
½ cup oil

- Place sugar with scant 1 cup water in a pan over moderate heat and stir till dissolved. Raise heat and boil till it reaches the thread consistency. (A little syrup poured into a cup of cold water forms a thin thread.)
- Add coconut and keep stirring till it turns dry.
- Mix eggs with cardamom powder and mix in, continuing to stir constantly till dry again, and remove from heat.
- Peel plantains and slice lengthwise without separating them.
- Place coconut mixture between the 2 halves of each plantain and press lightly to close plantain.
- Mix together flour, salt and scant ½ cup water to make a thick batter.
- Heat oil in a kadhai, dip plantains in batter and deep fry in batches till golden.

MADHURA KOZHUKKATTA
Rice Dumplings with Coconut and Jaggery

Serves: 12

1 kg parboiled rice
1 tbsp ghee
1 medium-sized, fresh coconut, grated
Syrup made from 1 kg jaggery (see p. 33)

- Wash rice and soak in water for 3 hours. Drain and grind with 1½ cups water to a thick paste.
- Heat ghee in a pan, add coconut and jaggery syrup, and cook, stirring constantly, till dry.
- Allow to cool, pinch off lime-sized portions of rice paste and flatten it in your palm. Put 2 tbsp coconut-jaggery mixture in the centre, and work paste around to cover filling completely. Shape into round dumplings.
- Steam dumplings for 10 minutes.

ELLUM SHARKARAYUM CHERTHA AVAL UNDA
Parched Rice Sweet with Sesame Seeds

Serves: 8

1 tsp + 1 tsp ghee
250 gms parched rice (see p. 22)
100 gms white sesame seeds (til)
Syrup made from 250 gms jaggery (see p. 33)
½ medium-sized, fresh coconut, grated
3 tsp lime juice

- Heat 1 tsp ghee in a frying pan and sauté rice for 10 minutes. Remove from pan and set aside.
- Add remaining ghee to pan, heat through and fry sesame seeds for 10 minutes, stirring frequently. Set aside.
- Place jaggery syrup in a pan over moderate heat. Add coconut and lime juice, and cook till it thickens.
- Remove from heat and add rice and half the sesame seeds. Mix well, allow to cool and shape into lime-sized balls.
- Spread remaining sesame seeds on a plate. Roll rice balls on the plate coating them with sesame seeds.
- Store in an airtight container.

MUTTA MARICHATHU
Baked Eggs

Serves: 4

A Muslim dish.

This recipe, and the four that follow, call for baking. The traditional method was to convert the cooking utensil itself into an oven by placing red-hot coals above and below it. Hence, the lid of the utensil should be flat-bottomed with a ridge to keep the coal from falling off.

10 eggs, lightly beaten
1 cup sugar
3 white cardamoms, powdered
1 tbsp ghee
2 shallots, chopped

- Beat eggs with sugar and cardamom powder in a bowl till light and fluffy.
- Heat ghee in a frying pan, add shallots and fry for about 3 minutes till golden.
- Stir in eggs and remove pan from heat.
- Cover pan with a flat lid which has a ridge. Keep red-hot coals over the lid for 20 minutes and for 2-3 minutes below the pan. You can also bake it in an oven pre-heated to 180°C (350°F) for 5 minutes.
- Cool, unmould and serve.

THARIPPOLA
Semolina Cake

Serves: 4

A Muslim dish.

½ tbsp + ½ tbsp ghee
½ tbsp sultanas (kishmish)
½ tbsp unsalted cashewnuts
2 eggs, lightly beaten
⅓ cup sugar
100 gms semolina (sooji/rava)
3 white cardamoms, powdered

• Heat ½ tbsp ghee in a pan, add sultanas and fry till they puff up. Remove from pan, drain and set aside. Add cashewnuts and fry till golden brown. Set aside pan.
• Beat eggs and sugar well in a bowl till light and fluffy.
• Add semolina and beat again to make a paste.
• Stir in cardamom powder and reserved sultanas and cashewnuts with ghee.
• Heat remaining ghee in a pan, add to semolina paste and mix well.
• Cover pan with a flat lid which has a ridge and cook for 30 minutes with hot coals on the lid and low heat below. You can also bake it in an oven pre-heated to 180°C (350°F) for 10-15 minutes.
• Cool, unmould and serve.

KALTHAPPAM
Rice Cake with Jaggery

Serves: 6

A Muslim dish.

2¼ cups rice
Syrup made from 500 gms jaggery (see p. 33)
A pinch of salt
4 tbsp oil
¼ medium-sized, fresh coconut, chopped
4 shallots, chopped
5 white cardamoms, powdered

- Wash rice and soak in water for 3 hours. Drain, dry and grind to a fine powder. Sift twice to get a smooth powder.
- Add jaggery syrup and salt to rice flour. Mix well to make a smooth paste.
- Heat oil in a frying pan, add coconut and fry till golden brown, stirring constantly. Remove from oil and mix with rice-jaggery paste.
- Add shallots to pan and fry till brown. Mix into rice-jaggery paste.
- Sprinkle in cardamom powder, mix well and pour mixture into a round pan.
- Cover pan with a flat lid which has a ridge, and cook for 30 minutes with hot coals on the lid and low heat below. You can also bake it in an oven pre-heated to 180°C (350°F) for 20 minutes.
- Cool, unmould and serve.

MUTTA PATHIRI
Egg Pathiri

Serves: 6

A Muslim dish.

2 cups plain flour (maida)
5 + 10 eggs
8 white cardamoms, powdered
¼ cup + ½ cup sugar
½ cup ghee
100 gms unsalted cashewnuts
100 gms sultanas (kishmish)
50 gms poppy seeds (khus-khus)

- Knead flour with ¾ cup water to a smooth dough.
- Pinch off lime-sized balls of dough dust with extra flour and roll into thin, 10-cm round pathiri.
- Heat a tava, spread a little ghee on both sides of pathiri and cook till golden brown on both sides.
- Beat 5 eggs in a bowl, add cardamom powder and ¼ cup sugar, and beat well. Pour into a hot frying pan and cook, stirring constantly to scramble mixture.
- Beat 10 eggs with remaining sugar to make a batter.
- Spread ghee on the base of a frying pan. Dip a pathiri in batter. Lay it flat on the frying pan. Spread a layer of cashewnuts, sultanas, poppy seeds and scrambled eggs. Cover with another pathiri dipped in batter and repeat the layering, ending with a pathiri on top.
- Spread remaining batter on top and pour over remaining ghee.
- Cover frying pan with a flat lid which has a ridge. Place red-hot coals on the lid for 15 minutes and for

2 minutes below the frying pan. You can also bake it in an oven pre-heated to 180°C (350°F) for 20 minutes.
- Cool, unmould, separate pathiri and serve.

KADALAPARIPPU PATHIRI
Husked Bengal Gram Pathiri

Serves: 6

A Muslim dish.

4 tbsp husked Bengal gram (chana dal)
1 cup milk
15 eggs, lightly beaten
1¼ cups sugar
4 white cardamoms, powdered

- Wash gram and cook in ¾ cup water till tender.
- Drain and grind to a fine paste with milk.
- Beat eggs with sugar and cardamom powder, and mix into gram paste to make a dough.
- Pinch off lime-sized balls of dough and roll into thin, 10-cm round pathiri.
- Place pathiri in a pan, side by side in overlapping layers and cover pan with a flat lid which has a ridge. Keep red-hot coals for 15 minutes on the lid and for 2 minutes below the pan. You can also bake it in an oven pre-heated to 180°C (350°F) for 20 minutes.
- Cool, unmould, separate pathiri, and serve.

ETTANGADI
Dry-roasted Vegetables in Jaggery Syrup

Serves: 8

This sweet dish is specially made for the Thiruvathira festival.

The literal translation of ettangadi is 'eight markets'. Presumably, this strange name came from the fact that some of the ingredients are purchased from the market and not grown at home!

100 gms elephant foot yam (zimikand)
100 gms Malabar catmint (koorka)
100 gms colocasia (arbi)
100 gms yam (chupri aloo)
100 gms unripe plantain
100 gms cherukizhangu (chhota rathalu)
3 tbsp red cowpeas (lobia)
3 tbsp horsegram (kulthi ki dana)
1 ripe plantain
1 tender coconut
Syrup made from 1 tsp grated jaggery (see p. 33)

- Clean, peel and dry roast all vegetables over red-hot coals. Cut them into 1-cm pieces.
- Dry roast cowpeas and horsegram individually over low heat till they are cooked.
- Peel ripe plantain and cut into 1-cm pieces.
- Scoop out the flesh of tender coconut and cut it into 1-cm pieces.
- Place jaggery syrup in a pan over moderate heat. Add all ingredients. Mix well and remove from heat.

Note: Cherukizhangu is a small yam that is about 9 cm in length. Its thin skin has a few spikes that are not sharp.

ACHAPPAM
Rice Cookies with Coconut Milk

Serves: 6

A Christian dish.

You will need an achappam mould to prepare this dish.

500 gms sifted rice flour (sift through a fine-meshed sieve and use only the finest flour)
¾ cup coconut milk (1st extract; see p. 20)
2 eggs, lightly beaten
2 tsp sesame seeds (til)
½ tsp salt
2 tsp sugar
1 cup oil

- Mix rice flour with coconut milk in a bowl to make a batter.
- Add eggs, sesame seeds and salt, and mix well.
- Add sugar a little at a time, mixing it in well between each addition.
- Heat oil in a kadhai. Place an achappam mould in the oil. When mould is hot remove it from oil and dip into batter. Ensure that batter covers only ¾ of the mould.
- Remove mould and dip into hot oil. When the batter is cooked it will detach itself from the mould and fall into the oil. Turn it over so that all the sides are cooked.
- When achappam is browned evenly remove from oil, drain well and place on kitchen paper to absorb excess oil.
- Achappam can be eaten fresh or stored in airtight containers.

261

THENGPAPAL CHERTHA ARI HALVA
Rice Halva with Coconut Milk

Serves: 12

Halva with its west Asian antecedents is an important sweet dish for the Malabar Muslims. In fact, a key road in Calicut is called Sweetmeat Street (popularly known as SM Street) after the halva shops that lined its sides once upon a time.

1 kg rice flour
2 litres coconut milk (1st extract; see p. 20)
2 kg sugar
½ tsp salt
2 tbsp ghee
4 white cardamoms, powdered
100 gms unsalted cashewnuts
100 gms sultanas (kishmish)
1 tsp rose-water

- Mix rice flour with coconut milk in a pan. Add sugar and salt, and cook, stirring continuously, till it has the consistency of a very thick porridge.
- Stir in ghee, cardamom powder, cashewnuts and sultanas. Continue cooking and stirring till it begins to solidify.
- Sprinkle in rose-water, mix well and remove from heat.
- Spread on a flat greased tray, allow to cool and cut into squares.

CHAKKAPAZHAM VARATIATHU
Jackfruit Halva

Serves: 12

½ cup ghee
100 gms unsalted, split cashewnuts
2 kg ripe jackfruit
Syrup made from 1 kg jaggery (see p. 33)
4 white cardamoms, powdered

- Heat 1 tbsp ghee in a frying pan, add cashewnuts, fry till brown and set aside with ghee in the pan.
- Clean jackfruit and remove seeds. Chop flesh into very small pieces and place in a pan with jaggery syrup and 1 litre water. Place pan over moderate heat and cook, stirring continuously.
- When water has evaporated, add remaining ghee and continue cooking till mixture thickens to the consistency of a heavy dough.
- Add cardamom powder and reserved cashewnuts with the ghee in the frying pan, and cook till halva solidifies.
- Spread on a flat greased tray, allow to cool and cut into squares.

Variation: Instead of jackfruit, ripe banana can be used. Sugar can also be substituted for jaggery syrup.

KASUANDIPARIPPU CHERTHA THENGA HALVA
Cashewnut and Coconut Halva

Serves: 4

1 medium-sized, fresh coconut
1 cup ghee
500 gms unsalted, split cashewnuts
1 kg sugar
6 white cardamoms, powdered
½ tsp nutmeg powder

- Cut coconut into very tiny pieces.
- Heat ghee in a frying pan and fry coconut till brown, stirring constantly. Remove from pan, drain and set aside.
- Add cashewnuts to pan and fry till brown. Remove from heat and set aside with ghee in the pan.
- Place sugar and 1½ cups water in a fresh pan. Place over moderate heat and stir till sugar has dissolved. Bring to boil and boil to the thread stage. (A little syrup poured into a cup of cold water will form a thin thread.)
- Add reserved coconut and cashewnuts with ghee from pan, and keep stirring and cooking till it solidifies.
- Sprinkle in cardamom and nutmeg powders, mix well and remove from heat.
- Spread on a flat greased tray, allow to cool and cut into squares.

THENGA HALVA
Coconut Halva

Serves: 6

2½ cups coconut milk (1st extract; see p. 20)
1¼ cups milk
1¼ cups sugar
½ medium-sized, fresh coconut, grated
50 gms unsalted butter

- Mix coconut milk with milk in a pan and bring to boil. Add sugar and grated coconut, and continue cooking, stirring continuously till it solidifies.
- Mix in butter and remove from heat.
- Spread on a flat greased tray, allow to cool and cut into squares.

NENTHRAPAZHAM CHERTHA THENGA HALVA
Plantain and Coconut Halva

Serves: 6

8 ripe plantains
¾ tbsp + 1¼ tbsp ghee
1 medium-sized, fresh coconut, grated
2½ cups sugar
1½ cups milk

- Steam plantains for 10 minutes, peel and mash.
- Heat ¾ tbsp ghee in a frying pan, add coconut and fry till brown, stirring constantly. Remove from heat and set aside with ghee in the pan.
- Place plantains, sugar, milk and remaining ghee in a pan and cook till it begins to thicken, stirring constantly.
- Add coconut and continue to cook and stir till it thickens to the consistency of a very thick porridge.
- Remove from heat, spread on a flat greased tray, allow to cool and cut into squares.

SHARKKARA UPPERI
Jaggery-coated Plantain Chips

Makes: 1 kg

Served at feasts.

1 kg unripe plantains
2½ cups oil
Syrup made from 750 gms jaggery (see p. 33)
1 tsp ginger powder (saunth)
3 tbsp sugar

- Peel plantains and split into half lengthwise. Cut each portion into 1-cm thick half circles.
- Heat oil in a kadhai and deep fry chips in batches till crisp and golden. Remove from oil, drain and allow to cool.
- Mix jaggery syrup, ginger powder and sugar in a pan, and cook till syrup reaches the soft-ball stage. (A little syrup poured into a cup of cold water forms a soft ball.)
- Add fried chips, mix well to coat evenly, remove from syrup and spread on a tray to dry.
- Cool and store in an airtight container.

KAYA VARUTHATHU
Plantain Chips

Makes: 500 gms

Plantain chips are usually cut into thin rounds.

Besides this well-known variety, the plantain can also be cut into half centimetre thick slices which are then quartered and fried. Both types are served at feasts.

1 kg unripe plantains
½ tsp turmeric powder
2 tsp salt
2½ cups oil

- Peel plantains and cut into thin round slices.
- Heat oil in a kadhai and sprinkle in turmeric and salt.
- Fry chips in batches till golden and crisp.
- Remove from oil, drain, cool and store in an airtight container.

Variation: **Chena Upperi (Elephant Foot Yam Chips)**: Cut yam into 1-cm cubes. Do not add turmeric and salt to oil before frying. Halfway through frying, sprinkle in a few drops of salt solution made with 2 tsp salt dissolved in 4 tbsp water. Cool and serve immediately. In this case coconut oil enhances the flavour. These chips are also served at feasts.

KOZHUKKATTA
Savoury Rice Dumplings with Coconut

Serves: 12

**1 kg parboiled rice
2 medium-sized, fresh coconuts, grated
1 tsp salt**

- Wash rice and soak in water for 3 hours. Drain and grind with 1½ cups water to a thick paste.
- Grind coconut with salt coarsely. Add to rice paste and mix well.
- Pinch off orange-sized portions of rice paste and shape into round dumplings.
- Boil 5 litres of water in a pan and drop dumplings into the boiling water. Cook for 15 minutes, remove from water and drain well.
- The dumplings can also be placed on banana leaves and steamed for 10 minutes.

KALLUMMEKAYA NIRACHU
VARUTHATHU
Deep-fried Stuffed Mussels

Serves: 8

A Muslim dish.

1 kg mussels
1 tbsp red chilli powder
1 tsp fennel seeds (badi saunf), powdered
1 tsp salt
1 cup oil

Filling:

1 kg (5 cups) parboiled rice
1 medium-sized, fresh coconut, grated
8 shallots, chopped
A pinch of cumin seeds
1 tsp salt

- Wash rice for filling and soak in hot water for 8 hours.
- Drain and grind all ingredients for filling to a thick paste with 2 cups water.
- Wash and scrub mussels well. With a sharp knife, scrape off the poisonous beards and filaments at the joints of the shell. Wash again.
- Place mussels in a pan with water to cover and boil for 30 minutes. Drain and prise open shells with the edge of a knife, without separating the shells.
- Rinse in fresh water and drain thoroughly.
- Fill opened mussels with filling and steam for 15 minutes. Allow to cool and remove shells.

- Mix chilli powder, fennel and salt with ¾ cup water.
- Dip mussels into paste and marinate for 15 minutes.
- Heat oil in a kadhai and deep fry mussels till golden brown.
- Drain and serve.

Note: Discard any mussels that are not tightly shut.

KALLUMMEKAYA VARATHATHU
Deep Fried Spicy Mussels

Serves: 8

A Muslim dish.

1 kg mussels
½ cup oil

Ground to a fine paste:
3-cm piece ginger, chopped
8 cloves garlic, chopped
4 tbsp red chilli powder
¼ tsp cumin seeds
2 tsp salt
4 tsp water

- Wash and scrub mussels well. With a sharp knife, scrape off the poisonous beards and filaments at the joints of the shell. Wash again.
- Place mussels in a pan with water to cover and boil for 30 minutes. Drain and prise open shells with the edge of a knife. Discard shells, rinse mussels in fresh water and drain well.
- Rub spice paste into mussels and marinate for 15 minutes.
- Heat oil in a kadhai and deep fry mussels for about 10 minutes till golden.
- Drain and serve.

Note: Discard any mussels that are not tightly shut.

KALLUMMEKAYA ADA
Mussel-filled Pastry

Serves: 4

A Muslim dish.

250 gms mussels
2 tsp + 1 cup oil
3 medium-sized onions, chopped
6 green chillies, chopped
3-cm piece ginger, chopped
1 stalk curry leaves, chopped
¼ tsp turmeric powder
1 tsp red chilli powder
½ tsp Malayali five-spice powder (see p. 32)
1 tsp black pepper powder
½ tsp salt
2 cups plain flour (maida)

- Wash and scrub mussels well. With a sharp knife, scrape off the poisonous beards and filaments at the joints of the shell. Wash again.
- Place mussels in a pan with water to cover and boil for 30 minutes. Drain and prise open shells with the edge of a knife. Rinse mussels in fresh water and drain.
- Heat 2 tsp oil in a pan, add onions and fry till brown. Reduce heat, mix in green chillies, ginger and curry leaves, and fry for 2 minutes.
- Add mussels, spice powders and salt, and fry, stirring constantly, till completely dry. Remove from heat and set aside.
- Mix flour with ¾ cup water and knead to a soft, pliable dough. Pinch off lime-sized portions of dough and roll

273

into rounds, 10-cm in diameter.

- Place 1 tbsp filling in the centre of each round and fold over edges to cover filling and form a square. Press dough lightly to seal.
- Heat 1 cup oil in a kadhai and deep fry pastries in batches till golden brown. Drain and serve.

Note: Discard any mussels that are not tightly shut.

Variation: Minced chicken, mutton, beef or crabmeat can be substituted for mussels.

KALLUMMEKAYA UNDA
Steamed Mussel Dumplings

Serves: 8

A Muslim dish.

50 mussels
1 medium-sized, fresh coconut, grated
2 medium-sized onions, chopped
3 cloves garlic, chopped
2 stalks curry leaves, chopped
1 tbsp red chilli powder
1 tsp salt
1 tbsp oil
1 tsp mustard seeds

Wrapping:

1 kg (5 cups) parboiled rice
½ tsp salt

- Wash rice for wrapping and soak in hot water for 8 hours. Drain and grind with salt and 2 cups water. Set aside.
- Wash and scrub mussels well. With a sharp knife, scrape off the poisonous beards and filaments at the joints of the shell. Wash again.
- Place mussels in a pan with water to cover and boil for 30 minutes. Drain mussels and prise open shells with the edge of a sharp knife. Rinse mussels in fresh water, drain well and cut into 2-3 pieces.
- Mix mussels with coconut, onions, garlic, curry leaves, chilli powder and salt.
- Heat oil in a pan and sprinkle in mustard seeds. When

they start sputtering, add mussel-coconut mixture and fry for 5 minutes, stirring occasionally.
- Add scant ½ cup water and cook till dry. (If there is excess water wrap mixture in a thin muslin cloth to absorb it.)
- Rub your hands with oil and pinch off lime-sized portions of rice paste. Flatten and place 1 tbsp of mussel-coconut mixture in the centre. Work wrapping around to cover filling completely and shape into a round dumpling.
- Steam dumplings for 15 minutes.

Note: Discard any mussels that are not tightly shut.

Variation: Minced chicken, mutton, beef or crabmeat can be substituted for mussels.

Glossary

English	Scientific	Malayalam	Hindi
Amaranthus	Amaranthus hybridus	Chuvanna cheera	Cholai
Asafoetida	Ferula asafoetida	Kayam	Hing
Ashgourd	Benicasa hispida	Kumbalanga	Petha
Banana	Musa sapientium	Pazham	Kela
–flower		Vazhakudappan	Mocha
Beef		Mattirachi	Gai ka gosht
Bengal gram	Cicer arietnum	Kadala	Chana
–husked		Kadalaparippu	Chana dal
–whole			Kala chana
Bilimbi	Averrhoa bilimbi	Irumpanpuli	
Bittergourd	Momordica charantia	Pavakka	Karela
Black beans	Vigna mungo	Uzhunnu	Urad
–husked		Uzhunnuparippu	Urad dal
–whole			Sabut urad
Brain		Thalachor	Bheja
Breadfruit	Artocarpus incisa monoceros	Kadaplavin chakka	
Butter		Venna	Makkhan
–clarified		Ney	Ghee
Buttermilk		Moru	Chhaas
Cabbage	Brassica oleracea	Muttakoos	Band gobhi
Cambodge	Garcinia gummigutta	Kudampuli	Kaymboj
Caraway	Carum carvi	Seemajeerakam	Shah jeera
Cardamom			Elaichi
–white	Elettaria cardamomum	Elam	Chhoti/sufaid elaichi

English	Scientific	Malayalam	Hindi
Carrot	Daucus carota	Carrot	Gaajar
Cashewnut	Anacardium occidentale	Kasuandi	Kaju
Cauliflower	Brassica oleracea	Cauliflower	Phool gobhi
Chicken	Gallus gallus	Kozhi	Murghi
Chilli	Capsicum annum	Mulaku	Mirch
—dry red		Vattalmulaku	Sukha mirch
—green		Pachchamulaku	Hara mirch
Cinnamon	Cinnammomum zeylanicum	Karuvapatta	Dalchini
Clove	Syzygium aromaticum	Grambu	Laung
Coconut	Cocos nucifera		
—dry		Copra	Copra
—fresh		Thenga	Nariyal
—milk		Thengapal	Nariyal ka doodh
Colocasia	Colocasia esculenta	Chembu	Arbi
Coriander	Coriandum sativum	Kothamalli	Dhania
Cowpeas	Vigna unguiculatus	Payar	Lobia
Crab	Cancer pagurus	Njandu	Kekda
Cumin	Cuminum cyminum	Jeerakam	Jeera
Curd		Thairu	Dahi
Curry leaf	Murraya koenigki	Kariveppela	Kari patta
Date	Phoenix dactylifera	Eenthapazham	Khajoor
Drumstick	Moringa oleifera	Muringakayi	Surjan ki phalli
Duck	Anatidae	Thaaravu	Badak
Egg		Mutta	Anda
Fennel	Foeniculum vulgare	Perumjeerakam	Badi saunf
Fenugreek	Trigonella foenum-graecum	Uluva	Methi
French beans	Canavalia ensiformis	Beans	Fransbin
Garlic	Allium sativum	Velluthulli	Lasun
Ginger	Zingibar officnale		
—fresh		Inji	Adrak
—dry		Chukku	Saunth

English	Scientific	Malayalam	Hindi
Grapes	Vitis vinifera	Mundhiringa	Angoor
Green beans	Vigna radiata	Cherupayar	Moong
Hog plum/emblic gooseberry	Emblica officinalis	Nellika	Amla
Horsegram	Dolichos uniflorus	Muthira	Kulthi ki dana
Jackfruit	Artocarpus heterophyllus	Chakka	Kathal
Jaggery		Sharkkara	Gur
Kokum	Garcinia indica	Punampuli	Kokam
Lime	Citrus aurantifolia	Cherunaranga	Nimbu
Liver		Karal	Kaleji
Mace	Myristica fragrans	Jathipathri	Javitri
Malabar catmint/ coleus tuber	Coleus parviflours	Koorka	
Mango	Mangifera indica	Manga	Aam
Mussel/clam (hard/soft)	Mytilus edulis/ venus mercenaria/ mya arenaria	Kallummekaya	Shinanee
Mustard	Brassica nigra	Kaduku	Sarson/rai
Nutmeg	Myristica fragrans	Jathi	Jaiphal
Onion	Allium cepa	Ulli	Pyaz
Pearl spot	Etroplus suratensis	Karimeen	Kalundar
Pepper	Piper nigrum	Kurumulagu	Kali mirch
Pigeon peas	Cajanus cajan	Thuvara	Toover/arhar
Plantain	Musa pardisiaca	Kaya/Nenthrakaya	Katcha kela
Pomfret white/black	Pampus chinensis/ pampus niger	Avoli	Poplet/halwa
Poppy seed	Papaver somniferum	Kasakasa	Khus-khus
Pork		Panniirachi	Suvar ka gosht
Potato	Solanum tuberosum	Urulakhizhangu	Aloo
Prawn/shrimp	Palaemon serratus	Chemmeen	Jhinga
Red pumpkin	Cucurbita ficifolia	Mathanga	Kaddu/ seetaphul
Rose-water		Panineer	Gulabjal
Saffron	Crocus sativus	Kumkumappoovu	Kesar
Sardine	Clupea pichardus	Chala	Pedwa/taradi
Semolina		Rava	Sooji/rava
Sesame	Sesamum indicum	Ellu	Til

English	Scientific	Malayalam	Hindi
Shallot	Allium ascalonicum	Cheriya ulli	Sambar/Madras pyaz
Snakegourd	Trichosantes anguina	Padavalanga	Chirchinda
Squid	Loligo/ilex	Koonthal	Nal/narsingha
String beans	Vigna unguiculatus var. sesquipedalis	Achinga	Lobia
Sugar candy		Kalkandam	Misri
Sultana		Kismis	Kishmish
Tamarind	Tamarindus indicus	Vaallanpuli	Imli
Tapioca	Manihot esculenta	Kappa/maricheeni	
Turmeric	Curcuma long	Manjal	Haldi
Vermicelli		Semiya	Sevian
Vinegar		Chorukka	Sirca
Wheat	Triticum aestivum	Gothambu	Gehun
–refined flour		Maida	Maida
Yam	Dioscorea alata	Kachil	Chupri alu
–elephant foot yam	Amorphophallus campanulatus	Chena	Zimikand
–small yam	Dioscorea hamiltonii	Cherukizhangu	Chota rathalu
Yeast		Kanwam	Khameer

Sources: *Alan Davidson (2002); C. Madhavan Pillai (1976); Elizabeth Lambert Ortiz (1996); K.T. Achaya (1999); The Spices Board: List of Spices, Cochin; V.I. George: Commercial Fishes and Shell Fishes of India, MPEDA, Cochin, 1998.*

Select Bibliography

Alan Davidson, *The Penguin Companion to Food*, Penguin Books, London, 2002.

C. Madhavan Pillai, *NBS Malayalam – English Nighandu,* Sahitya Pravarthaka Sahakarana Sangham, Kottayam, 1976.

David Burton, *Savouring the East – Feasts and Stories from Istanbul to Bali,* Faber and Faber, London, 1997.

Elizabeth Lambert Ortiz, ed. , *The Encyclopedia of Herbs, Spices and Flavourings,* Dorling Kindersley, London, 1996.

Fred Fawcett, *Nambutiris – Notes on Some People of Malabar*, Madras Government Museum Bulletin, Vol. III, No. 1, Anthropology, 1900, Reprint: Asian Educational Services, New Delhi, 2001.

Gazetteer of India, *Kerala State Gazetteer, Vol. III,* Government of Kerala, Trivandum, 1989.

Jean-Anthelme Brillat-Savarin, *The Psysiology of Taste,* Penguin Books, London, 1994.

K.N. Narayana Pillai, *Swaadishta Paachakaraani,* Current Books, Kottayam, 1994.

K.M. Mathew (Mrs.), *Kerala Cookery,* Current Books, Kottayam, 1999.

K.T. Achaya, *A Historical Dictionary of Indian Food,* Oxford University Press, New Delhi, 1999.

K.T. Achaya, *Indian Food – A Historical Companion,* Oxford University Press, New Delhi, 1998.

Larousse Gastronomique, Paul Hamlyn, London, 1994.

M. Gangadharan, ed. , *The Land of Malabar, The Book of Duarte Barbose, Vol. II*, Making of Modern Keralam Source Series No. 1, Mahatma Gandhi University, Kottayam, 2000.

Nalini Sreedharan, *Grihalakshmi,* Sahitya Pravarthaka Sahakarana Sangham, Kottayam, 1993.

P. Bhaskaranunni, *Patthompatham Nootandile Keralam,* Kerala Sahitya Akademi, Trichur, 1988.

Tess Mallos, *The Complete Middle East Cookbook,* Parkway Publishing, London, 1996.

Thangam Philip, *Keralathinte Thanathu Pachakavithikal,* Bhashaposhimi (magazine), March 2002, Kottayam.

Umi Abdulla, *Malabar Muslim Cookery,* Orient Longman, Mumbai, 1999.

Index

Mutton:
- Attirachi Kari (Mutton Curry), 103
- Attirachi Peralen (Mutton Curry), 98
- Attirachi Thoran (Stir-fried Mince with Coconut), 102
- Thengapalum Thairum Chertha Attirachi Kari (Mutton Curry with Coconut Milk and Curd), 96

Mutton / beef:
- Irachi Chertha Kappa Puzhukku (Meat with Tapioca), 101
- Irachi Istoo (Meat Stew), 45
- Irachi Mapas (Meat Curry with Coconut Milk), 99
- Irachi Varutharachathu (Meat Cooked with Ground Coconut), 90
- Irachi Varathathu (Deep-fried Meat), 94
- Irachi Varatiathu – I (Meat Cooked with Chopped Coconut), 91
- Irachi Varatiathu – II (Meat Cooked with Milk), 93
- Thenga Aracha Irachi Kari (Meat Curry with Coconut), 95

Pork:
- Panniyirachi Kootan (Pork Curry), 111
- Panniyirachi Vindaloo (Pork Vindaloo), 109

MUSSELS
Varutharacha Kallummekaya Kari (Mussel Curry with Fried Coconut), 171

PICKLES
Ada Manga (Sun-dried Mango Pickle), 211
Chethumanga Kari (Chopped Mango Pickle), 207
Eenthapazhavum Narangayum Chertha Achar (Date and Lime Pickle), 218
Ennayillatha Manga Kari (Oil-free Mango Pickle), 214
Irachi Achar (Meat Pickle), 221
Kadumanga Kari – I (Oil-free Tender Mango Pickle), 208
Kadumanga Kari – II (Tender Mango Pickle with Fenugreek), 209
Kallummekaya Achar (Mussel Pickle), 223
Meen/Chemmeen Achar (Seafood Pickle), 222
Naranga Kari (Lime Pickle), 215
Nellika Kari (Amla Pickle), 219
Pavakka Kari (Bittergourd Pickle), 220

Thengapalum Pachha Kappangayum Chertha Chemmeen Kari (Prawn
    Curry with Unripe Papaya and Coconut Milk), 164

PRESERVES
Sharkkara Cherth Ada Manga (Sweet Mango Preserve), 206

RICE
Appam (Rice Pancakes with Coconut Milk), 187

Biryani:
- Irachi Biryani – I (Mutton Biryani with Coconut and Curd), 180
- Irachi Biryani – II (Mutton Biryani with Egg), 182
- Meen Biryani (Fish Biryani), 183

Cheerachoru (Rice with Amaranthus and Coconut), 187
Cheriya Ulliyum Thengayum Chertha Pathiri (Unleavened Rice Bread
    with Shallots and Coconut), 191
Idiappam (Rice String Hoppers), 189
Ney Pathiri (Unleavened Rice Bread with Ghee), 194
Neychhoru (Ghee Rice), 185
Pathiri (Unleavened Rice Bread), 191
Puttu (Steamed Rice with Coconut), 190
Puzhungu Pathiri (Unleavened Rice Bread Stuffed with Fish), 192
Thenga Chertha Pathiri (Unleavened Rice Bread with Coconut), 194
Thengachoru (Coconut Rice), 186

SAVOURIES
Chena Upperi (Elephant Foot Yam Chips), 268
Kallummekaya Ada (Mussel-filled Pastry), 273
Kallummekaya Nirachu Varuthathu (Deep-fried Stuffed Mussels), 270
Kallummekaya Unda (Steamed Mussel Dumplings), 275
Kallummekaya Varathathu (Deep Fried Spicy Mussels), 272
Kaya Varuthathu (Plantain Chips), 268
Kozhukkatta (Savoury Rice Dumplings with Coconut), 269

SQUID
Koonthal Varatiathu (Stir-fried Squid), 173

288   *The Essential Kerala Cookbook*

Tharippola (Semolina Cake), 256
Thenga Halva (Coconut Halva), 265
Thengpapal Chertha Ari Halva (Rice Halva with Coconut Milk), 262
Unnakkaya (Coconut-filled Plantain Fritters), 251
Unniappam (Fried Banana and Rice Sweet), 243
Valsan (Steamed Rice and Plantain Sweet), 242

VEGETABLES
Amaranthus (Cholai):
- Thengapal Chertha Cheera Kari (Amaranthus and Coconut Milk Curry), 49

Ashgourd (Petha):
- Kumbalanga Olan (Ashgourd Curry with Cowpeas and Coconut Milk), 50
- Kumbalanga Pulisseri (Ashgourd Curry with Buttermilk), 66

Aubergine (Baingan):
- Vazhuthananga Thoran (Stir-fried Aubergine with Coconut), 80

Bittergourd (Karela):
- Injium Thairum Chertha Pavakka Kari (Bittergourd Curry with Ginger and Curd), 62
- Pavaka Varathathu (Deep-fried Bittergourd), 65
- Pavakka Kichadi (Bittergourd Curry with Curd and Coconut), 55
- Pavakka Pachadi (Sautéed Bittergourd Curry with Curd and Coconut), 54
- Pavakka Theeyal (Bittergourd Curry with Fried Coconut), 57

Cabbage:
- Muttakoos Thoran (Stir-fried Cabbage with Coconut), 77

Cauliflower:
- Cauliflower Mezhukkupuratti (Stir-fried Cauliflower), 83

Colocasia (Arbi):
- Chembu Mezhukkupuratti (Stir-fried Colocasia), 84

Dal:
- Kadala Kari (Whole Bengal Gram Curry), 73

289

- Kootukari (Yam, Unripe Plantain and Bengal Gram Curry), 42
- Kumbalanga Olan (Ashgourd Curry with Cowpeas and Coconut Milk), 50
- Moloshyam (Spicy Pigeon Pea Curry with Vegetables), 71
- Pachakari Chertha Kadala Kari (Whole Bengal Gram Curry with Vegetables), 74
- Thenga Chertha Ulli Sambar (Shallot and Coconut Sambar), 68
- Thuvaraparippu Kari (Spicy Pigeon Pea Curry), 70

Drumstick (Sajjan ki Phalli):
- Muringakai Thoran (Stir-fried Drumsticks with Coconut), 81
- Muringakaya Mezhukkupuratti (Stir-fried Drumsticks), 85
- Muringakayum Mangayum Chertha Pachha Theeyal (Drumstick and Unripe Mango Curry with Coconut), 59
- Muringayila Kari (Drumstick Leaf Curry), 75
- Muringayila Thoran (Stir-fried Drumstick Leaves with Coconut), 81

Jackfruit (Kathal):
- Chakkakuru Thoran (Stir-fried Jackfruit Seeds with Coconut), 79
- Idichakka Thoran (Stir-fried Tender Jackfruit with Coconut), 80
- Thenga Chertha Chakkakuru Mezhukkupuratti (Stir-fried Jackfruit Seeds with Coconut), 84

Mango:
- Mampazha Kalan (Sweet Mango Curry with Curd and Coconut), 39
- Mampazha Pachadi (Ripe Mango Curry with Coconut), 53
- Manga Pachadi (Unripe Mango Curry with Curd and Coconut), 51

Mixed Vegetables:
- Avial (Mixed Vegetable Curry with Coconut and Curd), 48
- Moloshyam (Spicy Pigeon Pea Curry with Vegetables), 71
- Pachakari Chertha Kadala Kari (Whole Bengal Gram Curry with Vegetables), 74
- Pachakari Istoo (Mixed Vegetable Stew), 44
- Pazhavum Pachakariyum Chertha Pachadi (Fruit and Vegetable Curry with Curd and Coconut), 52
- Pulinkari (Sour Vegetable Curry), 56
- Thiruvathira Puzhukku (Vegetable Potage), 64
- Yogyarathna (Mixed Vegetable Curry with Coconut Milk), 67

Plantain:
- Erisseri (Yam and Unripe Plantain Curry with Fried Coconut), 41
- Kaya Mezhukkupuratti (Stir-fried Unripe Plantain), 82
- Kootukari (Yam, Unripe Plantain and Bengal Gram Curry), 42
- Kudappan Thoran (Stir-fried Banana Flower with Coconut), 78
- Nenthrakkaya Kalan (Unripe Plantain Curry with Curd and Coconut), 38

Potato:
- Istoo (Potato Stew), 44
- Thengayuam Puliyum Chertha Podimas (Mashed Potato with Coconut and Tamarind), 47
- Urulakizhangu Kari (Spicy Potato Curry), 76
- Urulakizhangu Podimas (Spicy Mashed Potato), 46
- Urulakizhangu Mapas (Potato Curry with Coconut Milk), 60

Pumpkin (Kaddu):
- Mathanga Olan (Pumpkin Curry with Coconut Milk), 50

Tapioca:
- Kappa Puzhukku (Tapioca Potage), 63

Yam (Zimikand):
- Erisseri (Yam and Unripe Plantain Curry with Fried Coconut), 41
- Kootukari (Yam, Unripe Plantain and Bengal Gram Curry), 42

WHEAT
Alisa (Chicken and Wheat Porridge), 195
Porotta, 196